Dedicated to children
and young people everywhere.
You are the future of the human race;
take it further.

More Laughter

Further Writings of

John Roland Stahl

Sixth Edition

updated October, 2018

ISBN: 978-0-945303-25-1

CONTENTS

Einstein's Fundamental Error .... page 9

One World Government .... page 13

Yet Another Letter to Barack Obama .... page 19

Is God Almighty?... page 22

Free Market Capitalism .... page 25

A Review of Zeitgeist, Moving Forward........................... page 30

Seven Ways to Retire the U.S. National Debt .... page 36

The Kabbalah and The Tree of Life................................. page 42

The Hierarchy of Importance... page 45

Retrospective... page 49

Re: The Happiness Project... page 56

A New Currency, A New Bank,
    and a New World... page 59

The War on Drugs.. page 64

A Congress of the Wealthy and Powerful .... page 67

The Falling Dollar, Continued.. page 70

Manipulated Markets.. page 74

Carbon Capture and Storage.. page 77

The Problem of Europe .... page 80

On Growing Old .... page 83

Money, Power, Politics, & God....................................... page 87

6

The Colors of the Aura .... page 94

Priests and Pedophiles .... page 115

A Modest Proposal to Achieve Peace
    in the Middle East .... page 129

Felix Polydactyl Meander .... page 135

Not Enough Love In the World .... page 139

A New Therapeutic Approach to Deviant or
    Criminal Behavior .... page 144

The Evolution of Theology .... page 147

Speculations on Cosmic Consciousness
    and the Love of God .... page 162

Philosophical Meditations
    on the Nature of God .... page 167

A One World Total Make-Over .... page 181

The Noosphere .... page 188

Economic Theory .... page 190

Tetragrammaton .... page 193

Guns or Money .... page 217

A Run on Uncle Sam? .... page 220

A Solution to the Fiasco of North Korea .... page 223

Geopolitics .... page 224

Korean Re-Unification .... page 226

Six Regions of the World
    on the Way to World Union .... page 228

The Apple of Discord ....page 232

Requiem for a Lost Planet ....page 236

Weapons of War ....page 240

Meditation on Consciousness ....page 242

Gravity ....page 247

The Religion Taboo...page 250

The Holy Ghost ....page 257

Uncertainty ....page 258

Proposed Address to the First Convocation of the

     Seminary of the Church of the Living Tree ....page 260

Endgame, USA? ....page 262

Einstein's Fundamental Error

March, 2010

I couldn't resist the title – I have recently seen an old Sherlock Holmes movie (*The Creeping Man*) in which some blowhard was just telling his secretary to announce the title of his talk at the next meeting of the Royal Society – "Darwin's Fundamental Error." I thought it was pretty funny.

Einstein's fundamental error was to assume that the speed of light were constant, among all the other measurements of time and space, motion and gravity.

"If time could change depending on your velocity, Einstein realized, then other quantities, such as length, matter, and energy, should also change. He found that the faster you moved, the more distances contracted (which is sometimes called the Lorentz-FitzGerald contraction). Similarly, the faster you moved, the heavier you became. (In fact, as you approached the speed of light, time would slow down to a stop, distances would contract to nothing, and your mass would become infinite, which are all absurd. This is the reason why you cannot break the light barrier, which is the ultimate speed limit in the universe.) . . . he also showed that matter and energy are unified and hence can change into each other." (from *Parallel Worlds*: a journey through creation, higher dimensions, and the future of the cosmos, by Michio Kaku)

"Einstein realized that matter and energy are just names for different descriptions of the same phenomena." (my edit)

I am thinking that the universe is filled with descriptions of phenomena all of which are relative to everything else. So why should the speed of light arbitrarily be determined to be constant? To be sure, any one concept can be considered to be constant, and everything else described around it, but that is like the Ptolemaic theory that the earth is stationary and the sun and planets revolve around it. I always thought it were arbitrary, and the earth could just as well be considered stationary as anything else – the Sun, for example. But we finally learn that all parts move within relative aspect of everything else, and that the speed of light is no more exempt from this "free float of currency" than anything else. You may peg all other currencies against the dollar, but, ultimately, the dollar, too, will be seen to hold a position towards all the other currencies which is, in fact, relative to them.

And, like Copernicus's alternative description of the movements of the heavenly bodies, of which the earth is just one more, led to simpler and more obvious descriptions of those movements, so, also, it may be found that there may be more illuminating ways of describing the events of our cosmos without adhering to the concept that the speed of light must always be assumed to be constant.

In fact, it seems to me, on the face of it, that Newton may have been more "correct" after all! I have always thought that "time" were not an observed phenomenon in the way that motion or even gravity may be – time is an arbitrarily applied yardstick by which other phenomena may be described relatively. It seems like a more intuitive way of looking at the movements of the heavenly bodies. Thus, instead of all the bending of time and space and motion and mass, you might have, in some descriptions of phenomena, situations in which it is the speed of light which goes "more quickly" or "more slowly" than other movement. Of course it is all relative, but that is not to say that Ptolemaic cosmology were equally as valid as Copernican cosmology – the use of Occam's razor to follow the simplest interpretation of events will lead us to the most efficient and beautiful explanations, which are rightly assumed to be the most useful indications (sidestepping altogether, as having essentially no particular meaning, the question of which description is "actually" the correct one).

Thus, reinterpreting all the most recent data from this perspective, allowing the speed of light to fluctuate just as much as any other measurement, depending upon which description appears to be the most useful, or the simplest, may yield a whole new metaphysics, or may simply re-instate Newtonian physics as it used to be before Einstein's interesting speculations. This is not to suggest discarding all of Einstein's work – it may be that his mathematical descriptions of the relationship between matter and energy be perfectly correct, but that it is just the assumption that the speed of light must be considered constant that is the applied hand-brake to the wheels when trying to understand the flow of events in the cosmos.

§

I may as well tackle gravity, too, while I am about it. I think that "gravity" does not describe some funny force that pulls objects together; but rather it is the other way around: the "Natural" state of the universe is Zero, pure nothingness. "Time is the measure of error." (from one of my earliest books, *Jokes*). Some force must be applied in order to create the Mother of all Distinctions which causes the undifferentiated universe to spring into being. This outwardly directed energy is the Yang aspect of God which created the cosmos at the Big Bang. So, when all of that energy which maintains the cosmos in a state of error, or manifestation ("All manifestation is error,' from the same book of *Jokes*) be finally dissipated, then the apparently discreet elements of which our universe be composed will finally contract together once again in the "final" (one more of a series, which may not necessarily be infinite in either direction) Singularity (the total Yin point opposed to the initial Yang). The fading of this energy (of maintaining the distinction/separation of parts) is observed as "gravity." The force of gravity will always be equal to all of the matter and energy of the cosmos, expressed as a function of time, or the speed of light.

As described in earlier articles (e.g., *Speculations on Cosmology*, reprinted in *The Laughter of God*), I imagine a series of "universes" blinking on and off as they pass through that Singularity. This sequence makes more sense to me than one enormous Big Bang which brought forth our Universe, fully formed, all at once, like Athena from the head of Zeus.

One World Government:

"The New World Order"

June, 2010

The subject of "One World Government" or "The New World Order" always seems to draw the most intense reaction from many people. "First we have genetically modified food, and then they're going to shove **One World Government** down our throats!"

I have mentioned this topic before; I freely confess that I repeat myself constantly. (Have I mentioned, lately, the incredible folly of cutting down the arboreal biological layer (trees) from the sphere of the earth? Unimaginable folly, probably dreamed up by the folks who advocate burning up your house to keep warm, or the hungry worm Ouroboros who relieves his hunger by eating its tail, or the government policy of spending their way out of debt.) If only people would pay attention to me the first time when I speak or write, then I wouldn't have to repeat myself so much.

What surprises me about this one is that my own considered opinion is that the One World Government is the single most important next step in the evolution of life on earth. I share this view with Pierre Teilhard de Chardin, Albert Einstein, Bertrand Russell, H. G. Wells, and a great many others, many of whom have probably been prominent members of the Illuminati, in one or another of its incarnations, while we're at it.

I would probably describe my political views to be somewhere to the left of radical, yet virtually the entirety of the Liberal Consensus seems to be agreed that the One World Government is THE most sinister manifestation of the machinations of the Illuminati Conspiracy, who are perceived to be a cabal of wealthy, powerful, or otherwise influential persons who are *attempting to participate in the direction of the evolution of life on earth.*

What?? Do you mean to tell me that there are actually people who are attempting to influence the evolution of life on earth?? What a fearful conspiracy!! And the wealthy and powerful, the ones whose decisions will most radically affect the flow of events, are actually in collusion with others equally or also wealthy and/or powerful, in efforts to distill their combined shared consciousness of what needs to be done? Are they trying to play God? Isn't the *Law of the Jungle* good enough for them?

What is God, anyway? Perhaps every element that contributes to the (higher) evolution of life is part of whatever God is. And, surrounding that, there is a vast field of inertia representing the opposition to the ordering influence of God. This energy which is evolving, which I am calling God, actually appears to be showing positive signs of being Alive!

Is this figure of a Creative and Positive Energy reaching out into new and unknown directions, and being surrounded by an inertia of chaos and randomness, an entirely new idea, or what? Oh, no – it is actually very, very old.

So why is everyone so afraid of this? I think the answer I hear most often is that everyone seems to be afraid that any time anyone or any group succeeds in obtaining power, they will invariably use it to further their own individual wealth and power, to the utter disregard of anyone else. If you look at the record of just about every known government, either in the present day, or in any of the known historical periods for which we have records, this accusation will be borne out with dead-on accuracy almost all of the time! With the possible exception of occasional enlightened emperors or despots, e.g.: Emperor Yao of ancient China, King Arthur of England (a legend will do quite as well as historical record – possibly better), Pericles of Athens, or Frederick the Great of Prussia, just about every king or ruler sets about collecting as much wealth as he possibly can for himself and his family as soon as he comes into power. Most rulers attempt to accomplish this by sleight of hand, but, more recently, rulers such as Ferdinand Marcos of the Philippines simply load up convoys of trucks with bars of gold bullion and trundle them right out of town. (Reported as a Joke.)

However, this universal drive to self-aggrandizement runs into a self-limiting factor: the higher you go in the ranks of wealth and power, the more radically and dramatically your priority shifts from acquiring more wealth to *preserving what you already have*. This is the classic Conservative, who has Made It, and doesn't want anything to change which might alter his status. But when you come to a pivotal position at the top, there is only one way to ensure the continuation of your own personal good fortune, and that is for the entire field of life energy world-wide to be operating with maximum harmony and efficiency, rather than, for example, war.

The second most common response to the concept of a One World Government is, "One World Government! But – but, that's *elitist*, and *paternalistic*!!" – the Elite, of course, being that famous cabal of wealth and power sometimes assumed to be banded together into a group like the Illuminati.

Let us suppose we have managed to accomplish this fiendish plot, and a One World Government is now in place; but, surprisingly, they have allowed the people of the earth to choose the person at the top, the one who will have the greatest power, and the greatest responsibility, for affecting the evolution of the flow of life on earth.

There are quite a number of candidates, and the rules for working out run-off elections are quite complicated, in order to ensure that voters are able fully to vote their mind, knowing that if their vote is lost in the early stages of voting, they will be able to vote again from the remaining candidates until there is a final winner. Most of these early choices may be made at the time of the original voting. This is called "Instant Run-off Election," and it will soon be routinely used all the time everywhere. Because of the importance of the question, however, it will probably be necessary to have at least one secondary run-off vote, for which votes will be limited to the winners of the first primary vote.

Here are some of the more interesting Candidates:

First, there is the elitist and paternalistic candidate, a quiet little man of remarkable intelligence and extensive learning, giving him the manners of a university professor. He does not seem to be remarkable in any way, unless you listen to him closely. It is very easy for him to get lost among the great rabble of more noticeable Candidates:

There is, for example, Genghis Khan (we have managed to clone several candidates from surviving genetic material of old stock . . .), who mentions his considerable experience as qualification for the post.

Another fortunate success from our cloning tanks is Idi Amin, who has graciously accepted the nomination, and has agreed to accept the position, if elected.

Running against these formidable candidates is George W. Bush, who wishes to remind the voters of his membership in the Skull and Bones.

We wanted to offer the candidacy of Adolf Hitler, whom we had no trouble cloning back to full virulence; however, he declined the honor, out of fear for his life, preferring to hide where he is rather than consider any return to public office.

Another force to be reckoned with is the Ayatollah Khomeini, who would like nothing better than an opportunity of extending Sharia Law to the entirety of the human race.

There are plenty of other candidates, but these pretty well represent the field. We will announce the winners, from whom the candidates for the second round of voting will be drawn, as soon as the results are in.

So, what do I think about genetically modified food? In general, I am very much against it. I think that it is absolutely imperative to maintain a viable population of natural, open pollinated fruits, vegetables, grains, and, in fact, everything propagated from seed, not only food, but fiber crops, and crops grown for any other use. Whenever seed companies try to sell a new seed, whether it has been genetically modified or created from natural hybrids, they are looking for one quality of over-riding importance: the Number One required feature of any new seed is that if anyone try to plant (I am still trying to bring back the use of the subjunctive mood) the secondary seed which will be produced by the primary seed offered for sale, such seed will either fail to germinate entirely, or be of enfeebled and useless quality. This condition is the deal-breaker. No new seed has any chance of survival unless it meets this paradigm requirement.

Everyone should refuse to use seed of this kind; only use heirloom seed or seed which is open pollenated and will reproduce itself with natural seed. It is all of these "terminator genes" which should be outlawed. I hope everyone will refuse to use such seed ever again – by which I mean just about every seed commercially available except for the few sources selling "heirloom seeds" or the equivalent. New seed from natural hybrids can always be welcome, but only when they are stable strains.

But I stop short of asserting that genetic modification should never be considered for any reason. While I am not convinced of the value of any genetic modification program with which I am familiar, I retain an open mind about such a possibility, depending upon circumstances which might not be anticipated.

Yet Another Letter
to Barack Obama

September, 2010

Dear President Obama,

Surely you understand the problem: all of the seeds of economic despair have been sown by your predecessors, and you have inherited a bankrupt country. Make no mistake: while there remain many wealthy and powerful people and corporations in the United States, the country itself is way beyond bankrupt. The only reason the Chinese bankers do not refuse to renew their loans is because they, along with everyone else in the world, are terrified of the world which would follow after the United States is unable to meet its obligations. The nation has existed on credit for many years, tossing more trillions on top of the camel's back, because there doesn't seem to be any other option. The real problem is that the effects of fiscal policies are not really felt until twenty years after they have been implemented, yet a sitting president must defend his record every two years.

So you are reduced to only two options: either stand up sheepishly, like Gorbachev of the Soviet Union, and admit that the American System has fallen victim to its own success: the wealthy and powerful have become so wealthy and so powerful that they have been able to enrich themselves while impoverishing the country as well as the "little people," their less fortunate brethren. Then the American people can dissolve the Union, put a new government in its place, and repudiate the $12 trillion debt as the extravagance of the previous corrupt and bankrupt system in its dying days.

Or, you can begin to implement a serious program to pay off that debt. Forget about rampant poverty and unemployment — there is nothing you or anyone can do about that now. Contrary to the popular wisdom, flushing more money down the economic toilet will only make the problem worse, not better. The time when an influx of cash would buy another year or two at the expense of an ever more certain ultimate collapse is long gone. Scattering another trillion dollars into the wind will barely slow down the rapid collapse of the financial system. ("Trillion"? My goodness, how rapidly even the terms inflate: a few years ago, a billion dollars was "real money;" now, when speaking of throwing money into the wind, we would say, "a few trillion.")

There is only one policy that makes any sense: slash government spending and raise taxes, especially on the wealthiest segment of the population. Yes, this will plunge the country into a very deep, dark depression from which it may never recover, but a determination to pay down the debt is the only way to restore faith in the troubled American Dollar. This will mean that the United States will simply have to cancel all of its international adventures (read: "wars").

I have seen pie charts of the budget: it is basically divided into three large sections: 1. Defense (Orwell-speak for War); 2. Transfer payments to impoverished (or otherwise) Americans; 3. Service on the Debt. (Oh, yes, there is also one other tiny sliver: all other functions of government, but that doesn't amount to much.) If you elect not to let the Debt continue its spiral out of the world of reality into utter fantasy land, that leaves just the Department of "Defense," and the Transfer Payments. The Defense budget must be shrunk to just a tiny shadow of its current budget. The only way to do this is only to fund projects that are genuinely concerned with "defense", and curtail all activities of war.

As to those pesky transfer payments, I have had an idea many years ago which I still believe makes a lot of sense. The current system pays out checks beyond number so that recipients can rent a cheap hotel room in the city and spend their life drinking coffee (or beer) and smoking cigarettes. None of this makes any sense to me. I would propose that paying out cash money to all of those people is not only bankrupting the country, but it is also counter-productive. As an alternative, the nation should sponsor the establishment of Free Farms where impoverished people can go and live their lives in peace, with a place to sleep and food to eat. It will be incomparably cheaper to provide direct services of food and housing to people than to send out millions of dollars in welfare checks every month. It should also provide a better living environment for the poor.

None of this will be popular, and you will be hounded out of office at the end of your term, but that is going to happen anyway. At least if you launch programs that might save the country, then after another twenty or thirty years, the country might conceivably come out of its downward spiral and begin the long road back to prosperity. You may live long enough to be recognized as a Statesman after all.

Is God Almighty?

December, 2010

Any serious effort to discuss theology must begin with a rigorous analysis of all definitions involved in the discussion. It was the brilliant insight of Wittgenstein that when these definitions are exhaustively analyzed until total clarity has been achieved, the questions and problems will unravel themselves, and vanish. It is the disappearing knot trick.

Every "problem" in philosophy should simply melt away like last year's snow under the bright light of this process of analysis. Once "clarity" has been achieved, whatever has been under discussion will simply be reduced to "zero" (or "infinity;" the two terms mean the same thing). When the "joke" is explained that caused the divergence of the infinite wisdom into two opposite ideas, then once again "it is all one."

It is only after this process has really been wrung dry, that it is possible to examine the fragments that might remain and see if they constitute an idea or not. Is there any point at all, for example, of introducing a term such as "God" into the discussions of philosophy? Does the whole thing have any meaning, and if it do, then what be it? (This is the subjunctive mood again, Buster, and if you don't like it, just put up with it.)

There may be nearly as many ideas of what God is as there are people to wonder about it. There are many traditional definitions, but not really any final consensus; at least, not any consensus to which I am able to subscribe. One way that I see to express the answer to the question is to say that "God is what is left over when all jokes are explained and vanish."

Well, I have my idea of what is the most relevant and useful way to understand the ultimate resolution of this oldest of all problems, *"What is the Nature of God?"* But I want to compare that idea with some of the traditional definitions. If there be a proposed consensus, it seems to run along these lines: In the First place, it is the Agency by which the cosmos were created, or came into Being. Next, it is pretty universally presumed to be omnipotent and omniscient – all powerful and all knowing. Finally, it is asserted to be all good.

The fly in the ointment is the Problem of Evil. One way to express the Problem of Evil is, *"How can you believe in a merciful God when there are such creatures as mosquitoes on the earth?"* There are several other ways in which this problem is sometimes presented, but they all convey the same general idea.

I finally came to the conclusion that something had to go, and it was the idea that God were omnipotent. All of the other attributes are clear and wonderful, even obvious; but there is really no reason to introduce omnipotence among the other attributes of God. In fact, once you consider the aspect of a God which is a little more humble than previous incarnations, your admiration may clarify and greatly enlarge, not be reduced, by "such a come-down as to be giving up the claim to omnipotence."

Even the omniscience might be toned down a bit. The Omniscience of God is obviously the Collective Unconscious, as it was termed by Carl

Jung, or the Mind of Gaia, or Cosmic Consciousness, as others describe it. God is Life, and Life is Consciousness. The more life, the more consciousness; and the more consciousness, the more life. However, vast as this Ocean of Consciousness may be, we can only speculate as to its limits.

Even the assumption that it must be "good" must be looked at very carefully to be sure we understand what we mean by "good." Is Life as a whole more interested in the survival and enlargement in the whole field of life energy, or does it favor any one part of that ocean of life? To put it bluntly, is Man favored of God, or what?

I don't present my arguments here; I only present my conclusions. The ideas and arguments are far too complex to put into words, and I don't want to make that effort, but I think the human race does represent a very mature development of the energy of life, and, as such, its survival will always be a major part of the agenda of life. However, the survival of the trees may overshadow the importance of man; if the planet becomes uninhabitable, the race of man cannot survive.

The most pressing problem on Gaia's agenda is to reverse the physical decline of the earth. Since Gaia (or God) be not omnipotent, it must be up to Us Who are actually God, after all, to take upon Ourselves this responsibility.

Free Market Capitalism

February, 2011

Somewhere I think I mentioned an annoyance I felt when an American President is talking about his goals of spreading democracy, when, of course, his goals had nothing to do with democracy. The United States may be some kind of a democracy, but that is not what gives it its defining character. The American Way of Life has always been about Freedom. Not only political freedom or religious freedom, but economic freedom. It is a system in which everyone is free to throw up his own carnival tent and hawk any wares he pleases. The Glory Days of the patent medicines were finally shut down by the food and drug laws, and many other little prohibitions and taxes are trying to rein in some other abuses, but, to a very large degree, Americans are free to do what they want in pursuit of economic gain, with very little regulation.

This is Free Market Capitalism, and it isn't necessarily a bad thing, but it can sometimes lead to excess and abuse, and sometimes even to excessive abuse. In the case of the military involvement of United States forces, within the memory of the last twenty or thirty years, their purpose has had nothing to do with democracy (this has been shown too many times to review here), but everything to do with maintaining a *status quo* which will not interfere with the capital interests of the United States Corporations, which is to make as much money as they can.

The problem is that the moving directive for the whole show is to make as much money as you can. On a global scale, this is just no longer an acceptable option. There are some very real and pressing problems threatening the survival of life on Earth, and the world-wide tensions and instabilities all over the globe just make the problem of planetary survival almost impossible to cope with. When it comes to burning up the rain forest, the profit motive just won't do, any more.

And I don't mean to single out the Americans – anyone who has enough money to join the club, meaning that you have enough money or power so that it matters to the Earth what you do with it – is automatically a member of the same club. Go ahead; try to get as much as you can for yourself before the music stops.

The whole planet must be cultivated as the single field of biological energy that it is. Once this is accomplished, the problems facing our survival can be dealt with, at least as the start of an on-going effort, within one or two generations. But without it, the survival of human life on Earth is seriously threatened.

Ecosystems are just as fragile as economies. We have seen, historically, how massive panics have set off long periods of economic depression: just a few things get out of whack, and the whole thing collapses. Life is very similar! When an organism's living environment is radically damaged, its survival is threatened. We know what we, as a species, have to do. Lester Brown sums up the problems and reasonable solutions in his book, *World on the Edge*. The problem is that there is no money in it. All the money and power in the world is on the other side!

I have always laughed at people who get hysterical with conspiracy theories when they suggest that the people with money and power are actually running the world. Of course the people with money and power are running the world! Oh, it gets shaken up every now and then with a revolution, which might be bloody, as in the French Revolution, or nonviolent, as the liberation of India from England. But, by and large, it is fairly well established that the people with the money and the power use that money and power to retain the money and the power in the hands of – themselves, the people with the money and power. Now, is that ever a tautology, or what?

This leaves us with two opposing camps, with quite different agendas. In order for life on Earth to survive, we have to convince the people with the money and power that the survival of life on Earth is worth their serious consideration. In fact, if political changes could be made that would ensure the ease of addressing survival concerns (yes, that would be some form of the dreaded *One World Government*), that should make for a Golden Age of free trade.

The problem is that a very significant portion of the world's wealth is directly related to the maintenance of a perpetual war footing. Why has no one mentioned George Orwell lately? The perpetual war, for manipulating the people and also to profit from war industries, was a central feature of Orwell's world in *1984*.

None of those huge industries are going to be at all happy with a world in which their services are no longer required. So, while some elements of the money and the power in the world might support an initiative that would allow life to continue on Earth, the industries of Destruction will oppose, to the death of the last man, anything that would reduce the amount of warfare going on in the world.

That sounds like a problem. I'm going to have to think about this for a while.

We need a different model of how to regulate this world of ours. The jungle of sovereign states, sovereign corporations, and sovereign individuals stomping around can no longer be tolerated. (As Lily Tomlin says, "This is the *Phone Company!* We are omnipotent.")

I want to establish a seat of authority: the voice of God. I literally want to incarnate God on Earth, as the chosen One of a special seminary of candidates, who will be given the very best education with emphasis on History and International Studies. The idea is simple enough: any reasonably competent person could handle the tasks required of him, to arbitrate in cases where no other satisfactory decision can be found. But we give the Authority to the Seminary as a whole, not to any one individual. It is up to the Seminary to nominate the One who will interpret and exercise the Will of God as Steward of the Earth.

We have the confidence that, as a school, they will know which one of their number to choose for the stewardship. It is a microcosm: a little world, in which the solutions to the problems of the greater world can be found. (It is simply an alchemical vessel, to those who are students of Hermetic philosophy.) There is even the additional consideration of the effect of world opinion: the energy from these other sources can contribute to the channelings of energy that could result in the manifestation of an incarnation of God. Maybe the world actually works this way, and together We can focus our energies upon our alchemical vessel and cause a manifestation of an incarnation of God to appear on Earth to lead us forward.

The role of this person would be to maintain an overview of the whole planet, with the responsibility of keeping it all alive and healthy. Such an institution doesn't have to have any legal basis at all, and a fully endowed School of International Studies could be assembled of young people selected from all over the world for the purpose of creating a kind of "alchemical vessel" from which a manifestation of God were expected to emanate. The entire school would continue their specialized study of world affairs, and would constitute the most trusted sources from which the Speaker would draw information for making his calls. Whether this institution would ever attain a political influence is unpredictable, but here is a model in which I would place my trust ahead of any other schemes of which I have heard.

But, once again, I see that I have bridged the gap – there is no reason to suppose that those who are profiting from plundering the Earth and laying it waste will voluntarily cease and desist, with or without a court order. So what can we do, here? I have put it in theological terms because it amounts to nothing less. The source of authority is the power of God. If the project works as expected, there may be a real expectation that an incarnation of God may appear, and when One is anointed, perhaps the Glory of God will fall upon Him. That's what we need – we need God to come again upon the Earth and guide us how to proceed with our stewardship of the Earth.

If the Seminary be given this mission, it will create a very powerful field of magical energy around it, and God will appear.

A Review of Zeitgeist, Moving Forward

February, 2011

"You can only get a loan from a bank
if you can prove that you don't need it."

I have been watching *Zeitgeist, Moving Forward,* and it is pretty interesting – lots of ideas sound familiar to me from my own writings, but there is one very critical point, which they seem to miss, and it surprises me.

The whole discussion of "access centers" where you just go in, take what you need, and when you are done you simply return it – all for free, etc., is appallingly simplistic. The narrator dismisses the notion rather quickly that if everything be freely provided, everyone will simply lie in the sun and do nothing.

My own insight is that this whole idea is subject to severe limitations, and even then it is suitable only for a certain segment of the population. I envision a two-tier economic system to accommodate both sharpeners and levelers – a free market economy for the upper tier (limited by what I have called a "resource depletion tax"), and a "free farm" arrangement for the poorer members of society (*vide: New Solutions to the Problems of the Present Day - a Plan for International Prosperity and World Peace,* 1992, reprinted in

The Laughter of God). The problem is how to deal with poverty, because the free market capitalist economy does not adequately provide for the social problems of poverty. On the other hand, the free farm approach encounters serious obstacles when it is attempted to apply it to all of society: it runs counter to the desire inherent in all of life to flourish and "get ahead."

I hardly need to detail the flaws in the *Zeitgeist* (or free farm) approach to economics: no one will want brand B; everyone will want the best of everything, the newest, biggest, and best. No one will want anything used, chipped, older, outmoded – there will be no economic incentive for selecting anything other than the very best of everything. Why eat hamburger and fries when you can eat lobster and caviar?

No, my system allows for providing for the needs of the poor with a free farm arrangement, but there will have to be a certain amount of regulation in the distribution of "free goods." For one thing, I imagine two tiers to provide a minimal, but essential degree of regulation: an upper tier of "stewards" who form the responsible core of the farm and who enjoy a somewhat better standard of living than the "volunteers." For example, the better living quarters, better quality beds and so on, will be given for the use of the stewards, while the older stuff (or smaller rooms) will be given to the volunteers, perhaps on a seniority basis. Anyone who wants anything more will have to pay for it. Of course, the funny notion of "no longer observing money" is so simplistic that I hardly need to pass over that with more than a tolerant smirk, and I have already exceeded my quota.

So, instead of paying out millions of dollars every month in transfer payments so that the idle poor can occupy a room in a flophouse downtown and spend their days smoking cigarettes and drinking coffee, we can simply provide space at one of the country farms where these people can be provided for in a humane way, yet at the least cost to the rest of society. This will leave the cities as spaces occupied only by those who are actually involved in productive work. When a business fails, you don't have to resort to crime and fraud – you can simply pack it in and chill out at the free farm until you (perhaps with a different set of partners) feel like taking on another project "off the farm" and "into the jungle."

The cost to society will be hugely less (free farm *vs.* transfer payments) for two reasons: direct costs will be far less; a hundred people can be kept in decent comfort on the free farm, with dormitories and cafeterias, for the cost of a few welfare checks. But, secondarily, the immense social costs of robbery, fraud, marketing of useless junk, drug addiction, prostitution, murder, and other by-products of a necessity to come up with money every month, will be greatly reduced, since there will be no need for any of that behavior. (It won't be eliminated entirely, of course, because there are other causative elements apart from financial necessity.)

But it is an essential part of my vision that this whole free farm culture exist side by side with a free market capitalism, so that everyone can be as free as they want, but with another option for those who wish to get off the tread-wheel for a while. The other half – those in the free market who are motivated and on to something, will find they can accomplish their goals in a streamlined manner, without being bogged down by carrying all the dead weight of loafers or drunks.

I see plenty of utopian visions like that suggested in *Zeitgeist*, but I have never seen anyone advocate anything like a two-tier system which combines socialist utopian theory with free market capitalism. It has always seemed interesting to me that the idea is a perfect marriage of Capitalism and Communism, both of which have some interesting and commendable features, but both of which are plagued with some very serious problems. Socialist utopian visions can never work unless a creative element is free to explode off the top, providing evolutionary vitality. The Social Contract should provide for both Sharpeners and Levelers.

Oh, and, by the way, all the malarkey about the insidious monetary system with its debt basis seems to be misapplied emphasis. The real lesson there is that debt is a killer, whether it is personal debt, corporate debt, or the national debt of a sovereign state! Once you are in debt, and must borrow more money at ever more punishing terms in order to keep afloat, it becomes harder and harder to keep from sliding ever more deeply into debt. In fact, you are not expected to get out of debt; the plot is to run people into debt so that they cannot avoid financial collapse, during which time the banks continue to claim their confiscatory 29% interest for the five or six years it may take for foreclosure proceedings to close.

In the same way, on the other side of the interest pay window, once you have sufficient wealth it is easy for that money to earn more wealth faster than you can spend it, causing a continuous rise in personal wealth. Once you reach a certain plateau, then the inertia is all behind you to become more and more wealthy. It is a mirror image of The Descent Into Hell whereby your increasing debt level forces you inexorably past the line into realms where the laws of mathematics will force you ever deeper into the hole until you reach a point where it is impossible to recover (legally – of course there will always remain the options of murder, mayhem, fraud, and theft, not to mention prostitution, drugs, and gambling).

This is inherently and progressively unfair, and it leads to social stratification with a self-perpetuating wealthy class over an endlessly struggling class of peons who can never get out of debt (as Alice learned through the looking glass, "you have to run very fast just to stay in the same place"), unless they are fortunate enough to hit upon some winning strategy, or join a successful revolution (not a bad option to consider, these days). It is unfair to blame the bankers who offer loans at high interest rates: the high rates are required to cover the significant default rate on the shakier loans, so that the worse your financial status, the more interest you have to pay to service your debt. Banks are not really responsible for debt: they simply take advantage of it to make money. One solution would be to outlaw the loaning of money at interest, so that no one would be able to get into debt. This has been tried, with usury laws forbidding the charging of more than 10% interest, for example. This makes sense: if your credit is so bad that no one will risk lending money to you at less than 10% interest, it probably means that you are fundamentally bankrupt, and the circulations of debt simply postpone the inevitable collapse and give much of the profits from your collapse to the bankers instead of your final creditors. You might as well simply bail out and go to the free farm as hang on another few years with escalating debt levels until the inevitable collapse.

Borrowing money at interest is a very scary business, whether for a person, corporation, or sovereign state. The risks and dangers of falling behind and reaching a level where it is mathematically impossible to recover are very real. The consequences can be far-reaching, whether it be the bankruptcy of personal family finances, the bankruptcy of General Motors, or the bankruptcy of Iceland, Ireland, Greece, or Spain, followed, like dominoes, by all the other countries until China is left alone on the

Monopoly board as the winner – and then there will be another revolution and someone else will rise to the top. I don't think this transition has been adequately appreciated by the modern world: military might is no longer the real measure of power; it has given way to economic might.

The activities of the American government might seem to promote a growing economy with a growing GDP, but that is just the visible bubble on top: the underlying real financial strength is not measured in economic activity, but by more fundamental measures of wealth: actual resources, including natural resources, money (both held and owed), and infrastructure: schools, roads, hospitals, water, and power – Zeitgeist got that much right. The world is currently played like a game of Monopoly, and the United States is not necessarily winning the game; in fact, this should be a wake-up call, since there are still substantial resources remaining in that country, yet they are melting away very quickly under some very surprising economic theories. *(Will P.T. Barnum please stand up?)*

Actually, the "United States" is not really one of the players on the Monopoly board. There are numerous Players, both individual and corporate, but "The United States" is just a fictional abstraction (in financial terms, a scam). It is an imaginary sink into which debt is loaded, and this is one of the principle mechanisms of generating more wealth for the Players, as the "U.S. Government" sinks woefully beyond that line of total bankruptcy to a mathematical certainty, barring the fortunes of war, and/or acts of God. The country has been played like a Ponzi scheme for the last hundred years, and Uncle Sam is wearing The Emperor's New Clothes.

On the other hand, it might start raining manna from Heaven any day now; I hope you have a bag ready.

Seven Ways to Retire the U.S. National Debt

March, 2011

Just recently I updated an article I wrote about four years ago: *The Fall of the Dollar* (reprinted in *The Laughter of God*). The original article, written in 2007, contained a graph of the U.S. National Debt from 1940 until 2005, which showed a rather sobering exponential curve, suggesting that there was no way it could go but up, up, up, at an ever accelerating pace, as is the usual case with exponential curves. The graph ended at 2005 showing a debt of about $7 trillion. I just updated the article to include an updated graph which carried the graph up to 2010, with the debt standing at about $14 trillion, neatly doubled over the last five years.

The point of that earlier article was that the only alternative to the collapsing value of the dollar was for the United States to embark upon a series of wars of conquest, rape, and pillage.

However, upon further consideration, I have come up with a total of seven strategies for retiring the U.S. National Debt:

1. Divine Intervention. This is the most optimistic scenario. Let us all pray for divine intervention to solve the economic problems of the American government. As I speculate upon this possibility, it occurs to me

that such divine intervention would most probably come as part of a larger package in which more than just American problems were addressed, but, as there are an unlimited number of ways in which such divine intervention might take place, further speculation along these lines would be fruitless. Rather than instructing God as to how we want Him to manage the rescue of the financial affairs of the U.S. government, it is perhaps more becoming of us humbly to ask Him to use His best judgment in these matters.

2. Inheritance. When an individual finds himself laboring under ever escalating levels of debt, far beyond any ability he might have of repaying those debts, he can always hope for the death of some wealthy relative who might leave a fortune to him, enough for him to pay off those debts. In the same way, perhaps the United States government might inherit that $14 trillion dollars from somewhere. Admittedly, this isn't very likely, and perhaps we are still best advised to pin our hopes (and our wagers) upon the first possibility: divine intervention. However, perhaps Saudi Arabia might decide to dissolve itself as a State, or at least to gift all of its oil fields to the United States government. It would not do, of course, for them to donate the oil fields to privately owned American corporations; no, in order for this possibility to offer any relief to the American government, it must be the U.S. government itself that would be the recipient of such a gift.

I do not have all of the numbers in hand, but perhaps such a gift might manage to float the United States over its current doldrums. On the other hand, such a gift might simply open the floodgates for massive new spending, which, if they are no more sensible than what we have seen over the last twenty or thirty years, might not even solve any problems at all. In fact, much like the stories of someone who inherits $20 million and then, through a series of bad decisions, rapidly runs through all of the money, ending up with massive debts far in excess of whatever debts he may have started with, this hypothetical gift of the Saudi oil fields might just make the American problems even worse. But, at least potentially, we must allow that such a windfall could be the means of rescuing the rapidly deteriorating financial prospects of the United States.

3. A third possibility is that the American government discovers some new source of wealth – perhaps gold mines located on federal lands. Once again, it would be useless for any of this to be discovered or owned by private individuals or corporations; in order for it to do the U.S. government any good, it must be a discovery on lands owned directly by the federal government. However, gold mines probably wouldn't work. If enough gold were discovered (in the Grand Canyon National Park, for example) to pay off the National Debt, the value of gold would collapse. If twice as much gold were to be found, to offset the collapsing value of the gold, that value would simply fall even faster – there may not be any quantity of gold that might make much difference, due to the inexorable law of diminishing returns.

However, there are other possibilities: perhaps some amazing new element were to be found that restores hair on bald heads, rejuvenates the sexual potency of aging men, restores beauty to aging women, and restores all functioning of the body to perfect radiant health indefinitely, allowing for theoretically infinite longevity (in the absence of any fatal accident). Some such discovery, as long as it were the sole monopoly of the U.S. government, might go very far towards reversing the slide to financial ruin.

4. Wars of Conquest. To say that there is substantial historical precedent for this method of restoring financial health to a failing state were to massively understate the case. However, let us hope, for the sake of future generations yet unborn, that the United States will not decide to go down this road. Let us all fervently hope that one of the other choices will prevail.

5. Revolution/Repudiation of the Debt. Now this is a promising possibility! Perhaps the American people, waking up to the fact that the wealth of the nation has been systematically looted by a handful of wealthy families over the past 235 years, finally decide not to take it anymore, and rise up and overthrow the corrupt regime, putting some new government in its place (after all, Thomas Jefferson suggested that a new revolution were required every twenty-seven years: every generation must arrange political affairs according to current realities). Then the new government might blandly say that the debts of the previous government were not theirs, and they disown any obligation to repay same. Of course, the present government might simply declare bankruptcy and likewise simply renounce all existing debt, hoping simply to carry on with business as usual, but, in practical terms, it is unlikely for such a declaration to go down very smoothly without a radical change of government from the ground up (i.e., from the People). This option, while perhaps able to accomplish its primary objective, is fraught with additional difficulties; however, the post–repudiation problems are beyond the scope of the present article.

6. Inflation/Collapse of the Value of the Dollar. This was the projected outcome of my previous article on the fall of the dollar: that the only really likely alternative to bankruptcy, financial chaos, and/or war is for

the value of the currency to be gradually eroded so that fixed dollar amounts are repaid with dollars which are worth substantially less.

7. A Tax on Wealth. Finally, among this catalog of unlikely alternatives, some of which might even appear to be frivolous suggestions, here is one more realistic (though highly improbable) option which could, theoretically, offer a real way out of the financial problems of the United States: put a tax where the money is! After all, it is largely due to the unconscionable looting of the financial resources of the country by the very wealthy that have caused the present desperate state of affairs, so it only makes sense that those American citizens and Corporations registered in the United States with huge piles of wealth stuffed in their mattresses should be the ones to pay up the bills of the country they have so sorely treated while the rest of the country's citizens have either been sleeping or been paid off.

In case you haven't figured it out yet, this option is the one that inspires me to revisit the financial problems of the dollar. The option may not be politically very popular among those with the wealth and the power in the country, but the other 98% of the population do still retain a theoretical legal right to enact such a tax. It may be possible, for example, to mount a popular campaign to achieve this goal of taxing the rich. Politicians might be elected on a platform of promising to vote for such an idea, and Congress might pass the necessary legislation to accomplish it. However, to avoid the rapid sheltering of funds, this would have to happen very quickly. Perhaps it might even be necessary to assess the tax rate retroactively to 2010. Large teams of special auditors would have to be employed to determine appropriate assessments. Criminal penalties (i.e. indefinite incarceration until and unless the tax were paid) would probably have to be imposed. We might even want to re-introduce the Guillotine.

Yes; the sharp ones among you will have noticed that these are not all uniquely different proposals. In fact, the present suggestion (of taxing the rich) is quite decidedly revolutionary. The fall of the Bastille in 1789 might meet its parallel in the fall of the House of J.P. Morgan Chase, for example. Additionally, the formidable political obstacles to such a course of action might require divine intervention after all. Thus, when making any wagers as to the probable outcome of the current financial *ancien regime*, be sure to draft the terms of your wagers very carefully to avoid disputes.

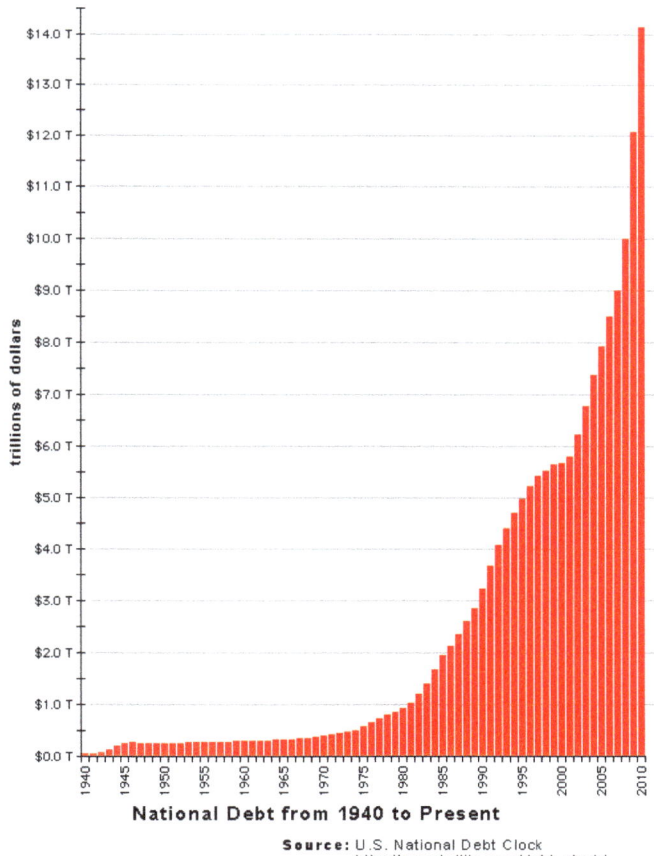

National Debt from 1940 to Present

Source: U.S. National Debt Clock
http://www.brillig.com/debt_clock/

The Kabbalah and The Tree of Life

March, 2011

I have studied eclectic philosophy all my life. I learned most about the Tree of Life of the Kabbalah when I accidentally re-invented it. When I saw that what I had done matched completely what was done before, I began to think that I must be on the right track.

It was Pythagoras who had the brilliant epiphany that the Numbers of mathematics are themselves the primary symbols of the Arcana, and comprise the original Metaphysics representing our Cosmos as Emanations from God. It is like all of the laws of geometry being based upon the definitions and axioms of Euclid.

Early on in my studies I figured out that all of the philosophies and religions in the world were all based around the same series of primary ideas, some emphasized more than others. I sorted out the ideas into those ideas expressed by the number One, ideas represented by the number Two, ideas illuminated by the number Three, ideas corresponding to the number Four, and ideas relating to the number Five. The meaning of each of these primary mysteries is best illuminated symbolically by the concept of the number associated with each idea *(Pythagorean Doctrine)*.

I developed simple images to illustrate the essence of each number, and this sequence of ideas represented by the numbers of mathematics formed the basis of my studies and teaching of Hermetic philosophy.

One day, pretty much by accident, I happened to stack my images vertically instead of horizontally, the way I had been presenting them in my books. To my surprise, I immediately recognized the Tree of Life from the Kabbalah. At first I thought this were an amusing coincidence, but, upon further investigation, I discovered that it was not simply the visible picture that was matched, but in every case, each of the 10 spheres *(Sephiroth)* corresponded precisely to the significance of the same position on my design! At first I was astonished, but eventually I realized that it would be more astonishing if they differed, since my sequence of images was intended to convey the same sequence of ideas represented by the Tree of Life: a primary Metaphysics illuminating evolution from God to Man.

After discovering this similarity, it became an easy matter to develop a much deeper understanding and appreciation of the Tree of Life. This is the same sequence of primary ideas as represented by every spiritual teaching in one way or another.

This primary sequence of Ideas and their Numbers from Pythagoras is none other than the Four Letters of the Name of God: *Tetragrammaton.* I was always very interested in the Tetragrammaton, as it was said to be the highest Key to understanding the Mysteries – the *Arcana.* However, all of my research sources lamented that the meaning and significance of the Tetragrammaton, while revered as surely the highest Key to the Mysteries, has, unfortunately, been lost. But such Mysteries cannot be lost. As Pythagoras tells us, the Illumination of each Mystery is contained within itself.

vide: Patterns of Illusion and Change, reprinted in *The Laughter of God.*

Yod **Arcanum I.**

Kether

☉

He **Arcanum II.**

Binah
Moon

Chokmah
Sun

SOLVE

Vau **Arcanum III.**

Geburah
Tamas

Chesed
Rajas

COAGULA

Tiphereth
Satva

He **Arcanum IV.**

Hod
Water

Netzach
Fire

Yesod
Air

Manifestation

Malkuth
Earth

The Tree of Life

The Hierarchy of Importance

June, 2011

The Hierarchy of Importance suggests an idea which comes very close to an illumination of the concept of God. It is of universal application: it is always invoked, in addition to anything else going on. When one searches philosophy for an answer to the questions of life, the function of the reply is to indicate that it is really the answer to the question, "What should I *do, now?*" That is really the answer behind every question; so what should I *do, now?*

Like everything else, the answer will unfold along the lines of that hierarchy of importance. What is of the most fundamental importance? I start with an understanding of our world as a single integrated field of life energy existing within the edges of chaos. What is important to understand is that it is a single organism, and that it is alive, and conscious. Perhaps it is linked with other patches of life energy in the universe, but, in any case, it is most useful to focus our attention upon the life we know of, here: Gaia, a personification of the living aspect of all of life on our planet Earth (God, to us).

Our hierarchy of importance starts with the survival and growth of this organism, which is *us,* after all. The major observation is that this field of life energy is under enormous, seemingly insurmountable, levels of stress; the planet has been visibly dying for several hundred years, and the pace of disintegration of the life force has picked up lately as the earth falls further and further behind, biologically.

Next in importance comes the consciousness that the biological condition of the earth needs to be turned around immediately, "at war-time speed," as Lester Brown says in his important book, *World on the Edge.* In fact, that book is an excellent place to begin learning about all of the problems facing the survival of life on earth, and some of the suggested ways of addressing those issues.

That book doesn't really consider the political issues, but there are very definitely political obstacles to the rapid and efficient management of the earth's resources back to a sustainable, and regenerative, level. So this next idea is the *One World Government,* as the political evolution most immediately essential for the regeneration of the earth to be undertaken. This is always the most politically charged proposal, but the only alternative to some form of *One World Government,* is a *Jungle of Sovereign States,* which is the political format which we are currently enjoying. At least, I suppose we are enjoying it. In the interests of a tight edit, I here omit a whole tirade upon the abuses borne by our Mother Earth by some of her Sovereign Masters, lately.

Moving right along, once we have a One World Government and a Single Currency, we will also want a standard and universal land tax, collected and administered by the State, but no other taxation, other than some sort of "resource depletion tax" which will be used to modify inappropriate activity for the earth.

Next in importance is to establish free farms for the indigent, world-wide. Everywhere in the world there should be places where anyone can go to live for free, with food to eat. This is by far the easiest way to deal with the problem of hungry people: just feed them!

At this point in the argument, it is time to address major issues in land use management in order to evolve ways of living on the earth which will tend to increase the life energy, order, and efficiency of life, rather than continuing the parade of its decline and death. It will come as a surprise to no one that I put the restoration of the Trees as first in importance under this heading!

But, not only do we need to plant more trees, we need to manage all of the biological cycles in the most efficient way, following the course recommended by nature. We will want to create healthy soil for restoring the earth to fertility, and an important example of what needs to be done is for all of the collection of residential organic waste (the toilet, plus kitchen scraps and yard waste) to be processed and returned to the soil in as short a loop as possible (whenever possible, all recycling should be done on the spot, *in situ*). All organic waste, from all sources, must be returned to the soil, or otherwise recycled into use. I have never believed that the entire whirlwind of waste processing is simply to throw it away. *As Above, So Below:* as it is in my garden, so it may be on the Earth: if I constantly recycle all organic waste back to my compost piles, active with worms, then I very quickly accumulate an abundance of rich soil which may be used to increase the coverage of my cultivation. But if the soil be depleted and dry, with flooding and soil erosion in other seasons, then the land will rapidly decline back to the desert.

The next in importance would be to establish a Seat of Authority behind the One World Government. My own idea is a Seminary of Candidates, a School of International Studies, which would collectively hold the Seat of Authority (*Throne,* or *Cathedra*), and which would endow one of their number as their Spokesperson, who would personally sign their decisions as their agent and advocate.

From here I see a great many lesser matters of process which seem to be flawed, and in need of correction of error. One of the most important ideas is the understanding of personal health in the same light as the health of Mother Earth, or Gaia. In order to ensure the survival of life on earth, we want to encourage all of the natural life processes to continue, and minimize interference from the forces of chaos. In the case of the soil of our earth, it is essential to cultivate her as an organic, living being, rich with life, and not clouded with chemical interference whose long term consequences are generally the opposite of the early experience (just exactly the same pattern as any other drug).

And we should treat our own body with the same reverence and respect, trying to understand how to maximize the integration of our life forces in accordance with the natural process, avoiding the use of synthetic chemicals. As our lands will become fertile again, our bodies will likewise become healthy and fertile again, and life can go on.

Retrospective

May, 2011

As my life passes in review before my eyes, I have to conclude that it has been a good life. I have made a great many mistakes, and much that I have attempted to accomplish remains unfinished. Perhaps some fresh young persons of a new generation may continue some of the work I have started, or realize some of my dreams, but, as for me, I will have to lay down my tools and allow the Evanescent Press to achieve its ultimate destiny of vanishing like a cloud of vapor, as my small contribution to the evolution of life passes into history.

All of my life I have looked at everything the way a proof-reader does – seeing the errors and looking for a better way. Sometimes this style might make it seem that I do not appreciate what is right and good, but that is not so: I love this world and this life; I love the people in our world, and I love the animals and the plants – my love of trees must be evident to anyone familiar with any of my writings. I have to admit that it is with a very great sadness that I let it all go when I fade away into oblivion.

But it is definitely true that I have a heightened awareness of error – I see it everywhere: in my own life, to begin with. I suppose my own mistakes and failures of judgment may not really be so much worse than those of most other people. I do not want to minimize my own errors – with my proof-reader's eyes it seems to me that I have done everything wrong. In my days as a letterpress printer on my handmade paper, I don't think I ever looked at a finished piece of work without thinking of some way in which I might have done it better: wider margins, a different font or size, different line spacing, or something. In the same way, I now look back upon time after time in which I made a bad choice or did something foolish or wrong.

Nonetheless, I am not afraid to stand in the presence of God and accept His judgment of my life. I have tried to do the best I could, and it seems to me that most of my errors were very small, though numerous. I recall little things: something I may have said to someone that I later realized must have been considered very rude – these are the things that torment me, not any really serious errors.

On the other side of the ledger, I consider what I have accomplished in my life. I have always considered my investigations into philosophy and metaphysics to have been of the greatest importance. I would say that my most important contribution to philosophy is my re-discovery of the significance and importance of the *Tetragrammaton* and the *Tree of Life* of the *Kabbalah*. This is followed, in my estimation, by my correlation of the primary trigrams of the *I Ching* with the planets and metals of astrology and alchemy and the colors of the aura. And in my later years, I have become more and more interested in the nature of Consciousness and its relationship with God.

Over the course of my investigations into the mysteries of philosophy and life, I have developed a complete system of metaphysics, which answers all of my questions about the ultimate nature of reality. My conclusions may be wrong, of course, or incomplete, but at least they satisfy my own requirements. One thing I have to admit is that I used to think I had a "complete" metaphysics worked out, and then I would evolve some new ideas which extended or enlarged the scope of my existing ideas. I conclude from that that I suppose that *it is only possible to know what we know; it is not possible to know what we don't know!*

However, at least I have answers which satisfy me for all of the principle questions of philosophy: the origin and nature of the world, and the meaning of God. I was puzzled by the Problem of Evil, until I finally figured out that "God" were not a Being of infinite and omnipotent power, but the collective consciousness of all of Life. All of Life: together We are God.

I should also say that I have not discovered anything new – I used to think I were formulating new and original ideas (in my youth), and then I read the *Tao Te Ching* by Lao Tzu, and I was amazed to find ideas there which I thought I had invented. Later on, after I had a whole metaphysics built up of a sequence of primary ideas, I discovered, in my life's major epiphany, that by arranging the symbols of my ideas in a vertical pattern instead of horizontal, I had reproduced exactly the *Tree of Life* of the *Kabbalah*. From there, I understood also the meaning of the *Tetragrammaton*, whose significance was said to be lost, but which was revered as the most important Key to the mysteries of life.

So I have not discovered anything new – all I have done is to have re-discovered for myself the meaning of the ancient mysteries. I have, however, arranged them all into a format which I believe clarifies their meaning better than anything I have seen presented anywhere else. All of these ideas are detailed in my earlier book *The Laughter of God*.

My understanding of God has evolved tremendously from my earliest efforts to understand things. At the age of six I experienced a theological crisis, since my father was a Methodist minister and yet as far as I could figure out it was all nonsense! I remained a confirmed atheist for most of my early years, yet I knew from the start that it were useless to denounce something as wrong without having an alternative to propose. Accordingly, I set about studying all ideas of philosophy and religion that I could find. I do not need to repeat the story of my growing understanding of those ideas, nor of the growing understanding of the nature of God, since it is all there in my published work, but I finally came around to appreciating the meaning and significance of God. At first, my idea of God was very abstract, but the more I continued with my investigations, the more I began to understand God in a more personal sense.

This all gets very complex. There is even a trinity of ideas that comprise my understanding of God: God the Father (or Mother) as the ultimate source and origin of the cosmos, which can only be seen in contrast with God the Son, an original movement out towards Novelty and Being. This may be understood as the original "joke" of imagining that Zero and Infinity mean different things. Our manifest cosmos represents the consequence of that original Joke, and the path towards reunion with God.

These "two persons of the Trinity" might be more easily understood as Female and Male principles, or Yin and Yang. But it is God the Holy Ghost which interests me lately: the God of the totality of Cosmic Consciousness that sustains and orders the evolutions of life on our world.

Looking at God in this way, and not as some all-powerful Being who is therefore responsible for all of the enormous errors and problems of the world, has encouraged me to understand the importance of Our own role: We are God, after all, and it is We who must take responsibility for the state of the world!

Instead of sitting back and "waiting for George to do it," We must shoulder the responsibility Ourselves! It is up to Us to evolve Our Consciousness towards union with God and lead the field of life energy out of Our current downward spiral and onto an upward path.

As I look over the last 10,000 years, it seems to me that there has been considerable positive evolution, and yet there are many very troubling signs in our current world. There are many who suppose that it is not possible to elevate the spiritual condition of Man or Beast, and that there is a fundamental selfishness that is inherent in the nature of life, but it is evident to me that there has been some real spiritual evolution going on. In fact, it has now become imperative for the human race (which, of course, occupies some of the higher ground in the hierarchies of Consciousness) to advance the pace of spiritual evolution if there is to be any hope for the survival of life on Earth.

I have tried to address some of these issues in my own life: my efforts to establish alternative sources of tree-free papermaking, utilizing abundant agricultural waste products instead of destroying the Trees of our ancient forest, have occupied most of the last fifteen years of my life. Even where annual fiber crops may be grown, hemp, for example, it will be the seed crop which will provide the primary harvest, yielding food for human nutrition, while the remaining stalks may be used for making pulp for paper. Many of these agricultural waste products are as good or better than wood as a source of papermaking, and there is already a great abundance of this material that is simply wasted and discarded every year.

And then, buried and forgotten among my older writings, there is my idea of a Seminary formed of young people selected from all over the world to form a school and training ground for leadership in addressing the problems of the world. I still think that this is one of the most important ideas I have offered, and that it has the potential to provide a framework by which we might evolve a better political structure for sorting out the problems of the world. This is, of course, a very tall order, but the current jungle of sovereign states, many controlled by cabals of greedy, ruthless, and very fearful men (they are mostly men) creates a very dangerous world which is beset by very severe problems which threaten the survival of life more than any other aspect of our world.

When I speak about "cabals of greedy, ruthless, and very fearful men," which countries do I have in mind? Well, just about all of them! Some are worse than others, but there are few governments that inspire much confidence. Problem states come to mind very easily, but whenever I am tempted to think of a country as rising above their more sordid neighbors, I am told by residents or nationals of those countries that the stink of corruption in their countries is as foul as anywhere else. I might be tempted to be more specific, but I think I prefer to keep the argument here very general.

Let us all hope and pray and work towards a better world. The first priority is to survive, and in order for the human race to survive, it is necessary for the planet to survive, and that means restoring the Trees, which have historically comprised the major portion of the Earth's living biological activity. The Trees have always been the primary basis of Life on this planet, and without them there is little hope for the rest of us.

Please, God, grant us the wisdom and the strength to do Thy will.

Re: The Happiness Project

September, 2011

I have studied philosophy all of my life, and I believe I have come to a clear understanding which I have tried to express as clearly as possible in my writings.

Among the many insights which a clear understanding of the principles of philosophy will provide is that Happiness is one of the expressions for that convergent point at the Center. If you imagine metaphysics to be represented by a sphere, there will be the convergent point at the center, which is infinite love, infinite happiness, total compassion, bliss, and joy, perfect radiant health, infinite energy, infinite peace, and infinite wealth, and everything good. As you move away from that point of perfection at the center, you move towards novelty, which becomes complexity, then confusion, and then chaos, at the periphery of the sphere, where the energy dissipates. This also means that as you drift further from that point at the center, you will have less energy, poorer health, increasing poverty, bewilderment, anger, and death.

I also want to mention that the search for Novelty is the spark of Life; the lesson here is that Novelty is only good up to a point; but Novelty is not the same as going bad. The *Solve et Coagula* of Hermetic Alchemy is the same movement away from the point, followed by a movement toward the point: a simple example is the action of a hammer. Or, in order to inhale again, you must first exhale.

This very simple concept can be used as a model by which to understand any process of change. For example, "a very simple measure of a person's level of spiritual growth is the degree to which they love everyone." Another way of saying the same thing is that "a measure of a person's level of spiritual growth is how happy they are." I prefer the former way of putting it, because if anyone wants to play the game of "more loving than thou," they are very welcome to do so! However, the game of being "happier than thou" doesn't seem to me to be nearly as much fun.

So the idea is not only that happiness is an important goal to be sought, but that the closer you get to the happiness goal (or the higher your "happiness quotient"), the more love you will feel, and the healthier and more beautiful you will be, *because it is all the same thing!*

So, like all other yogas, the Yoga of Happiness will bring you closer to union with God, and I'm all for it! This world needs all the happiness, and all of the love, that it can get.

Addendum appended for the rehabilitation of Timothy Leary:

There have been objections to Timothy Leary's slogan of "tune in, turn on, and drop out;" it seemed to be completely negative in its implication. However, I have long ago discovered the importance of considering an idea from the point of view of trying to understand what the idea was, rather than a literal interpretation of the words. In the present instance, Leary's idea is lost in the midst of its misconception. The first step towards a regeneration is a fall back. *Solve et Coagula.* Move back away from the forward point in any direction of novelty, followed by a renewed movement forward: Change is like the pounding of a hammer. Meditation is a similar *going within,* in contrast to the more usual *going out* that pervades so much of our life. Like a sabbatical, a period of going back may be followed by a creative and powerful movement forward: SOLVE ET COAGULA. So Leary's message can only be understood in the light of its obvious continuation: "and then do something New."

Tune in, turn on, drop out; and then do something new.

A New Currency, A New Bank, and a New World

September, 2011

Money is funny stuff. I think of it as one of the universal abstractions like "time" and "energy" or "power." They all mean the same thing; they are just different ways of looking at it.

Now that the world's financial structure has fallen apart, no one quite knows what to do. What do you do when a sovereign state goes broke, like Greece or the United States? And what is the role of Banks and Bankers? Who owns the money, anyway?

I have been under the opinion that the entire world needs a makeover in every sense. Like a great many others, I have realized that there can be no growth or movement forward in any significant way until the political unity of the entire world is settled.

That, in a nutshell, is the defining problem of our time. Whether or not human life, or any life at all, manages to survive the next hundred years will depend upon the way the people of the earth come to deal with this present crisis.

But that it is all One Ball of Wax is the first lesson; there is no point trying to patch up one hole here and stop another leak over there – the political problems facing the union of the planet are inextricably related to the economic problem, or the way in which the universal abstraction of Money will be applied to facilitate trade and prosperity.

This is such a huge problem and the objections against all of the solutions are legion, but I simply present it as self-evident that the planet we live on must evolve towards a political unity, or there is no hope for the survival of life. I spend no time debating the point; I just wish to lay out a vision of a way in which a new arrangement could work.

The entire jungle of currencies in the world and the complex web of financial entanglements linking them represent, in the most primary fashion, a description of the moving power of a living system. It is much like a schematic diagram of an electrically powered system. "Follow the Money."

I have considered the problem of the Source of Authority, and I have come to my own, perhaps surprising, idea of vesting that authority in a School, whose members would finally select the one to exercise the final authority. I have written about these ideas quite a bit for many years, but the function of this position has always confused and frightened people. It always seems to make them think that I want to endow some new Emperor with infinite power to lord it over the rest of us; when, in fact, of course, it is entirely the reverse: the whole necessity of a final Judge is to relieve us of the constant efforts, at every turn, of every man to get the most for himself (and the same goes for quite a few women, too). All the final judge would do would be to try to regulate the system as judiciously as possible to avoid all such excess and abuse.

But there is another very important aspect of this new world government: Money. One of the main roles of the Government would be to regulate the economy so that it functions with maximum efficiency, completely avoiding all such problems as are now overwhelming our current crop of world bankers, with their sovereign defaults upsetting a whole house of cards.

So, we start by issuing a new currency, which would replace all others currently in use. We call it the mammon, and we establish its value somewhere in the familiar range of the dollar, pound, franc, or euro. The Seat of Government would have the privilege and responsibility of printing and distributing this currency in such supply as would most effectively encourage efficiency in the market-place. That same Seat of Government would also levy a tax, based upon the ownership of land, and this tax would be paid in mammons. So this Seat of Government would actually be a World Bank, which would regulate the system of financial transactions worldwide.

The first step would be to calculate the value of the initial account each person (or corporation) would start out with. It would be the responsibility of this Bank and Government to determine and regulate these values.

That is the easy part. The harder part would be to liquidate the financial affairs of current governments. Essentially, each Sovereign State would be financially liquidated, and its value (or its debt) would be shared among the citizens of that State. This will not be easy! Next, as a consequence of that last effort, some people, from indebted countries like the United States, may end up with serious levels of debt. This is simply inefficient mathematically; it makes more sense to just give everyone else more money so that the poorest people end up with nothing, which is a great deal better than being in debt. If everyone's account were simultaneously raised by the amount of the largest debt, nothing would be changed in terms of the relationships between the accounts; we would simply have raised the line, so that we do not have to deal with negative accounts mathematically.

Yes, this Universal Account would also amount to a Universal Number! Everyone's worst fears would be realized: yes, there would be a New World Order, with a New Currency, a New Bank, a New Court, and a new King, and everyone will have a Number. Is this a vision of sheep lined up for slaughter, or is it a vision of the Golden Age, in which everyone lives happily ever after? Gone will be the rampaging bandits from the face of the earth, looting and pillaging as they go. In place would be a very simple system.

Anyone on earth who lacks the wherewithal to provide food, shelter, or health care could simply check into one of the Free Farms set up for this purpose, and their basic needs would be met. Everyone else would be free to work at any other occupation that they expect will provide them a better lifestyle than available at the Farm.

The Government could simply print up all the money it needs for this or any other purpose, since there will probably be a continuing need for more money going into circulation. Taxation on land would be the other alternative to printing money, depending upon the relative merits of each choice. There is no reason at all why there should be any problem with the Government simply printing up all of the money it needs to spend. Any time there ends up being too much money in circulation, the Government would simply reel it back in through taxation. In this way, a happy balance could be maintained, and life goes on.

A careful investigation into the consequences of such a system will reveal that it would be very, very efficient. For example, in the present system of taxation, a very large percentage of the total tax received is spent in preparing and calculating taxes, producing and distributing tax forms, auditing rogue corporations, collecting the tax, and hiring tax lawyers who attempt to minimize the tax owed by their clients. Under the system I envision, all taxes would simply be levied on the ownership of land. Once this were set up, the entire collection of taxes, world-wide, could be accomplished in a moment, in which everyone's calculated tax would simply be deducted from their account automatically, by computer programs. Of course, setting up and updating property values world-wide would be of central importance.

In the absence of wars or natural disasters, there is no reason why there could not be a continuing and rapidly increasing level of prosperity for everyone.

The War on Drugs

December, 2011

(a posting on a list:)

The War on Drugs:

Well, here are some references which relate to the Government's position on drugs:

www.naturalnews.com/034289_Afghanistan_opium_trade.html

Hello, Big Brother:

I have small expectation that you will allow this link to be published; bad enough that it has already been widely distributed on its own; better not let anyone who is involved in a more religious perspective (with a sacramental use of cannabis to get in touch with God), see any of this information!

Perhaps the articles are all wrong – how could our government be so single mindedly pursuing such an agenda of world domination, money, and power as to participate, gleefully, in the program of getting rich (so you can buy guns which you can sell in Mexico, Central America, or South America) while peddling heroin to inner city kids, to keep them sedated, with their minds off of revolution, just trying to get another fix?

Yet, out of the other side of their mouths, sipping their alcoholic drinks, they pursue an agenda targeting the use of cannabis, since most cannabis users are far more alternative- and counter- cultural than their martini sipping counterparts, most of whom can always be relied upon dutifully to support the Establishment.

And they still pretend that it is about Democracy, and not a program of financial and political dominance. And they blandly continue to use stock phrases like Freedom, Democracy, and the Bill of Rights, as if any of it had any meaning.

They ask the protestors Occupying Wall Street, "What are your demands?" Well, how's this for an answer: "We demand that everyone with Wealth or Power give away their wealth, abandon their power, and go jump in a lake!"

No? That one not going to work? Well, how about another idea: a Revolution of Everyone Else. Thomas Jefferson said that such a revolution should happen every twenty-seven years, in order to sweep away the accumulated concentrations of wealth and power, advantage and privilege. Perhaps a Revolution is overdue? Perhaps this will be a World-Wide Revolution, and Something Altogether Different will supervene?

Oh, no! There should be an immediate **Congress of the Wealthy and Powerful**, to consider how to deal with this threat.

Perhaps a constructive dialogue can be initiated in which the Congress of the Wealthy and Powerful try to negotiate a settlement with the World-Wide Revolution. Such a negotiated solution may be the only chance for the survival of life on earth.

And you can begin by lifting the ban on the freedom of speech. What have you got to lose? Isn't it better to let it go and see where it goes? I assure you, it is. Just let it go.

A Congress of the Wealthy and Powerful

(*Conclave at the Grotto*)

December, 2011

It is the worst fear of every conspiracy theorist: some Grand **Conclave at the Grotto** of all of the world's Wisest, Wealthiest, and/or most Powerful people, come to an emergency Congress to assess the state of the world, and the most immediate threats to the survival of life on the earth.

The dominance of the earth and its resources by the wealthy and powerful is not the only issue at stake: the biological survival of the thin envelope of life on earth, our tender biosphere, is seriously at risk. It is an essential and immediate necessity to address these problems. If we act fast, it may yet be possible for life to continue to exist on the fragile ecosphere and biosphere of our little planet.

But the problems extant on the world stage, if ranked by importance, look pretty bleak: not only is our fragile biosphere being rapidly degraded by unbelievably foolish and short sighted activities, but world-wide financial institutions, currencies, and balances of debt are out of control and spinning off into Chaos, with potentially dire consequences.

Underpinning all of this there is a very wild "Law of the Jungle" pervading throughout the earth, taking very frequently some very, very frightening directions. One loose cannon is enough to do significant damage to the Ship of State. But if the earth were covered with loose cannons – it is hardly necessary to mention any names! It is a much shorter list to come up with areas of the globe not under the dominance of one or more loose cannons.

The time has come to take the wraps off of what everyone has been warned is coming: **One World Government**. It is now time for those of wealth and power to convene a major Congress to determine how to implement the plan.

No one needs to be alarmed! Those of wealth and power will realize the importance of certain issues vital to the survival of life, so an orderly arrangement of those issues is the only sensible way to manage them, avoiding excess at all times.

Issues at stake will be the origin of the Authority for the executive responsibility, an agenda for the restoration of the biological health of the planet, the establishment of a new central bank for a universal world currency, the provision of a world-wide network of free farms for the housing, feeding, and care of the indigent, and such other issues as may be necessary of inclusion to an important new vision for the world, such as the imposition of a universal land tax to replace all of the whirlwind and confusion of taxes everywhere else, under and with which our world is mired and burdened.

The Number One Responsibility of the One World Government will be to protect and cultivate the Earth's biosphere as a garden, encouraging healthy survival and growth of the phenomenon of Life, world-wide. Perhaps next in importance will be the maintenance of the World Bank underpinning the new currency, for handling the matters of trade and finance. Since the "house" of the World Bank will be the One World Government itself, it can simply issue money as needed. A simple, universal land tax world-wide will replace all other instruments of taxation. (- with the exception of resource depletion taxes, which will have to be imposed upon an otherwise free market). Next will probably be the establishment of non-profit industries covering all essential aspects of civilization: food distribution, health care, transportation, and so on. Of course, the participation of anyone else or any other private company would be fully encouraged on a free market basis.

And that's about it: the limits of the new One World Government. Its issues are few, but important. Otherwise, it will also keep the Peace. This is a thankless job, and there will be endless disputes and protests, but any resolution of problems is better than a resort to arms, and all parties will benefit from a negotiated solution, even a "wrong" one.

Only a Congress of the Wealthy and Powerful will be able to bring about these changes. We cannot wait any longer before seriously addressing these issues. It is indeed a monumental task: it is nothing less than a complete makeover of the biological, political, financial, and social structures of the earth, but the survival of life on earth is at stake, and we have no other alternative but to take it on.

The Falling Dollar, Continued

December, 2011

I am not a politician, so I claim the privilege of changing my opinions whenever I wish. For the life of me, I cannot understand why it is held as such an essential virtue for a politician to retain an absolutely fixed and rigidly consistent view of everything. If there be no possibility for any evolutionary growth or change, then God help us all. I have far more respect for a politician who is able to follow an evolutionary path in the trend of his ideas and policies than for a politician who is stuck in the constipated cement of immutable dogma, built up brick by brick from his earliest public utterings.

I have been worried about the fate of the United States government and its people for a long time now. Of course, I have necessarily extended my concern to the entire human race, and the entire biosphere of the planet, commonly personified as Gaia, a conscious, living being. However, the United States is the biggest elephant in the room, and it appears to be stomping around beyond all control or reason, spinning off madly into chaos while the rest of the world watches, helplessly. Well, there is plenty of stomping around into chaos on all sides, but the American government is by far the largest and most powerful loose cannon on the deck of the world ship, and consequently is liable to do the most damage.

The heart of the problem is that the American government is so far beyond bankrupt that it is virtually a mathematical certainty for it to fail economically. Actually, of course, it has already "failed" long ago. It is like the original Carlo Ponzi, whose "Ponzi scheme" was utterly bankrupt for many years before the US government was finally able to force it down. The problem was that Ponzi was paying his high interest rates from the new funds which were constantly being subscribed! Since he kept on faithfully paying out those rates, people continued to re-invest and his empire was going on and on. Of course, mathematically this was untenable, and the longer it continued the greater the final devastation when it finally imploded.

My first article on the subject took it as understood that the only reasonable expectation was not for the government simply to declare bankruptcy, but, once no one else would take the risk of loaning it any more money, it would be forced simply to print up more and more dollars, driving the value of the dollar inexorably down and down.

My second article took another look at the problem and concluded that there was another option – that the United States tax the rich, whose looting of the treasury over the past 350 years has reduced the country to its present state of penury. This is politically untenable, of course, so it is not really much of a possibility.

But I have changed my opinion of what is to be done. In my last article on the subject, I detailed Seven Ways to Retire the US National Debt, introducing the option of taxing the rich. But I have reconsidered that approach in favor of a new option that I seem to have overlooked, probably because this new option is about as laughably impossible as taxing the rich. What if the US government should stop spending so much money? I will go out for coffee now, while everyone subsides into uncontrollable hilarity for the next twenty minutes. ("Does a bear shit in the woods?" they used to ask.)

It is not that it is even so impossible – I have already detailed a program of drastically curtailing spending – it is just that the nature of the beast is so rooted in endless, profligate spending that it is just unimaginable that there might be any way to curb the voracious appetite of this monster.

Still, if I am going to make any recommendations, I might as well, just for the record, suggest that the government quit spending so much money. Just to recap how to do this: no more wars, first of all. Free Farms instead of transfer payments. Simplify the tax code to consist of just a land tax plus a resource depletion tax. Eliminate about 90% of all federal jobs and bureaucracies, including the Department of "Defense." Put an end to the War on Drugs and other victimless crimes. Scrap endless regulation and "busy work." Oh, and pay off that debt as fast as possible.

There aren't enough jobs to go around anymore, but that should be good news – anyone put out of work by these policies could just go fishing, or retire to the Free Farm, and leave the rest of the economy to those who have something worthwhile to do.

Oh, yes – I really should address the objection that working people don't like the idea of supporting the poor. Why should someone spend a portion of his hard earned money to feed hungry people who don't have money of their own?

Well, in the spirit of Jonathan Swift's *Modest Proposal*, I might suggest a simple and elegant solution: every year, perhaps on January 1st, July 4th, or some other selected date, the poorest 10% of the world's population should be painlessly euthanized. This would not only go very far toward treating the problem of over-population, but what a stimulus to economic activity! Suddenly, all of those loafers who thought there were simply going to be fed humanely will be galvanized into action, and the race will be on.

As every year's losers are put out of their misery, the economy will start tightening up really quickly, freed up of all of that drag on the wheels of commerce.

Manipulated Markets

December, 2011

As we face the imminent collapse of the global financial system, credit markets, and currencies – not only the dollar and the euro; the whole concept of fiat currencies is being met with increasing skepticism – one thing is puzzling me: the collapse of the property markets.

Many people have been predicting economic chaos on a scale never before seen on earth, probably dwarfing the Great Depression of the 30s. As we face this possibility or probability, everyone wants to know how it will affect them, and how they can best manage their affairs to cushion the blow when it comes.

For the super rich, the problem is to find some safe assets to hold which will retain value after currencies become worthless. For everyone else, the problems are far more fundamental and primitive: what is the best way to ensure that you will have food to eat and a place to live?

For the rich, the solutions are precious few: gold and silver, perhaps, although these are not good long-term investments. Yes, a canny investment in precious metals (or even common metals, or other basic commodities) made at a carefully calculated moment has the potential to achieve a very satisfying return, but, long-term, the expense and hassle of holding gold or silver bogs down any realistic expectation of long-term growth.

It seems to me that the only obvious choice is land – the land of the earth is the ultimate source of value and wealth, and has been since the earliest times. But for ordinary people, too, ownership of land appears to be the safest investment in uncertain times. Even a very small piece of land could support a few fruit and nut trees. One English Walnut tree will provide major sustenance for a family forever. These tree crops should be supplemented with kitchen gardens of organically grown vegetables and berries. If your land has a natural source of water (and a mountain spring is more reliable than groundwater), you would be in a fair way to becoming sustainably independent. Add a solar power set-up and a good assortment of tools, and you should be able to survive nearly any upheaval.

So in the face of the natural value of land, particularly in times of trouble, the free-fall of the property market makes no sense to me at all. All I can think of is that the property markets are being deliberately manipulated so that "the smart money" can choose their moment and buy up all that land for pennies on the dollar, and then sit back while everything else collapses in value.

Here we have everyone in debt to the banks so they desperately try to sell off their land to pay their debts. The banks are already acquiring property rapidly through foreclosures; if someone were able to pay off their loan in cash, the bankers could then purchase other distressed property through the property markets. In any case, when the crash comes, do not be surprised if it is the banks, the bankers, and other custodians of "the smart money" who end up owning all the land.

Other than land, I really can't think of much else that would retain any value, with the possible exception of munitions factories, but I don't go there.

Carbon Capture and Storage

February, 2012

Once again they have been sitting up nights thinking up new ways of being stupid. I just don't understand how the same human race which has come up with some incredible stuff over the years can yet come up with something so bewilderingly stupid as the CCS plan – Carbon Capture and Storage (or Sequestration) as an antidote to the ravages of global warming. They tell me it will cost about $45 trillion to pay for it – I presume that tab will be covered from the U.S. government's current account surplus?

I read with growing disbelief that they are actually discussing gathering up CO_2, compressing it into liquid, and burying it in huge tanks in the ground, where it will be monitored for the next 10,000 years to prevent any toxic leaks. Is this a joke? Did I miss the laugh line? Is it a satire, something like Jonathan Swift's *Modest Proposal* (to eat the surplus children of poverty as a delicacy for the rich man's table)?

And here I thought everyone knew the obvious solution to the build-up of CO_2 – it is to plant trees all over the earth, so that they will sequester the carbon in a natural and even useful way.

While we are planting millions of acres of trees all over the earth, to sequester carbon, to stop soil erosion, to release oxygen, and to prevent seasonal flooding and drought, to shelter the earth below so that other plants, animals, and people can live a better life under their protection, why don't we plant tree crops – food trees – so that, in addition to all of the other benefits of the trees, we can put an end to world hunger and reverse the tide of disease that comes from eating excess meat and processed foods, laden with toxic chemical fertilizers and pesticides?

I want to plant endless plantations of fruit and nut trees – English walnuts, mangoes, avocados, cacao, apples, oranges, almonds, persimmons – yum! Even coffee trees! Hey, my information suggests that one or two cups of coffee (like one or two glasses of wine in the evening) will extend your life and improve your health; it is only in excess that it becomes a problem, exactly as is the case with alcohol, meat, salt, even sugar. While the trees are small, annual gardens of vegetables can be grown, or fiber crops such as hemp or kenaf for making paper – please: cutting down trees for pulp and paper is as barbaric as treating disease by bleeding the patient!

I don't even have to insist upon a purely vegetarian diet. I read all kinds of health information from all sources, and my conclusion is that you can pretty much eat anything, as long as it is not in excess! The American breakfast of steak and eggs with sausage and ham is too much meat (not to mention the chemicals and preservatives, but that's a separate issue). However, the Asian style of using small amounts of meat primarily as a flavoring to vegetables seems a bit less toxic to me. The large scale cultivation of animals for human consumption is a very expensive approach to human nutrition. The earth just isn't big enough to feed all the people on a diet heavy with meat. We can either cut back on the human population, reduce the dependence on meat, or both. A great deal can be accomplished simply by scaling back the role of meat in our diets. If there is an abundance of low cost fruits and vegetables available in the markets, then no one needs to go hungry.

What a simple and gentle solution! Stop global warming, feed the hungry, and save the world. What am I missing? Are the international bankers planning to loan us the $45 trillion for the CCS swindle? 99% of the earth (yes, *that* 99%) is already in debt to the Company Store, so what's the difference? Like the Greeks, we will all be slaves forevermore anyway.

However, Gaia, Mother Earth, is actually Mother Goose, laying golden eggs for us all. But if we kill the Earth and try to take all of the gold at once, we will all be dead, bankers and all, because we can't eat gold, and a dead Earth will no longer support life.

Therefore, choose Life.

The Problem of Europe

August, 2012

Today I read about the Problem of Europe as a question of creeping Federalism. Apparently Margret Thatcher anticipated the problem by saying that the only way the euro could work was by a form of increased Federalism, which she declared she totally rejected as unthinkable.

The economic problems of the euro are predictable enough when you try to have a single currency but multiple nations. The poverty and bankruptcy of Greece pale into insignificance when compared with the bankruptcy of the United States of America, yet the USA has one critical advantage over Greece: it can print up more dollars any time it wants (and, oh, does it want – and don't expect that thirst to be slaked any time soon), but Greece cannot print up more euros (unless no one notices as they slip some in – there's an idea).

It is easy to see the inevitability of the whole process, which has been going on for hundreds and thousands of years. Gradually, however long it takes, Europe will finally coalesce into a single entity, with a single currency. However, the same process will simply continue until, however long it takes, the whole world will finally become a single political entity, with a single government, a single currency, a single bank, and even a single language (probably English).

This may take anywhere from two or three hundred years to several millennia to work itself out into some sort of stable arrangement, but the world may not last that long. The biological survival of the Earth as a living organism, is a serious and open question. As Lester Brown (*World on the Edge*) and many others have concluded, it should be possible for the human race to intervene in time to save the Earth from dying out, but it is greatly complicated by the political chaos currently being enjoyed by the planet. Or not being enjoyed, as it may happen.

So why not simply fast-forward and get it done with right away, so that we can then proceed "at wartime speed," and with the very highest priority, to the process of reversing all of the many virulent processes killing off our world? Simple and obvious examples are the proliferation of toxic chemicals for the soil, and pharmaceutical drugs for human bodies. These must be replaced with organic processes and cycles if there is to be any hope for the survival of life on earth.

If all of Europe were united into a common land, with a single government and a single currency (but it is very hard to imagine a single language), that would probably provide significant benefits to all of Europe, including the wealthier parts which would eventually end up funding the elevation of the poorer parts. But the advantages gained would greatly outweigh these costs, which is why those wealthier nations and/or people will eventually pay the cost and unite Europe.

But all of that will only shift the argument and the problem to a larger theater: the World Stage. It is the Whole World that needs a single currency, a single bank, a single government, and a single language, not just Europe! Why do we waste our time in this way? The problem is urgent;

why don't we proceed immediately to a "Congress of the Wealthy and Powerful" to set up some protocol for advancing the argument? The sooner we accomplish those four Changes, the sooner we can all move on to the next and supremely important item on the Agenda: the survival of life on earth.

On Growing Old

October, 2012

I was going to say that growing old and dying are inevitable facts of life, but that is not right – dying is the inevitable fact of life, but growing old is an experience not given to everyone. I do not want to mention here by name all of those very dear friends of mine who have left the company of the living "way too soon," but some of them have left big, empty holes in my life, and they will live on in my memory for as long as I live.

Sometimes people ask me how old I am, and I long ago considered that a more relevant question was how many years of life and health do I have left? There are plenty of people in their twenties who seem to have less vitality remaining than I have, which is not to say that they will die sooner – I am very grateful for every morning in which the Sun rises yet again, covering this glorious earth with its warmth and sunshine. It is easy to see why the Sun has been the earliest aspect of nature worshipped as God. But we do not know the day or the hour of our own death, so we stop short of any such speculation.

But in the present essay I am not so much concerned with the physical deterioration of our body – I have observed that there seems to be a corresponding waning of life spirit as we grow older, and, just like the physical deterioration of the body, this waning of the spirit seems to be more accelerated in some than in others.

What is the single most defining characteristic of Youth? It is the Quest for Novelty, to discover or learn something new. It should not be necessary for the schoolmaster to force his pupils to learn; a good teacher need do nothing more than provide the resources and guidance for his students to pursue their own quest for learning. Rudolph Steiner understood this, and it is the basis of his Waldorf Schools. This is not to say that the teacher leans back and speaks only when spoken to! There are many ways in which a clever teacher can inspire his students on their paths of discovery, by introducing ideas and concepts to them in accordance with their interests.

And what is the single most defining characteristic of Age? Well, if I say that it is the waning of that interest in novelty, it must be understood that there are many wise men and women who retain their open and inquiring minds throughout their lives. I do not assert a cause and effect relationship for growing old and losing this interest in Novelty, but it might be suggested in either direction – that growing old causes one to lose interest in Novelty, or that losing an interest in Novelty causes one to grow old. They may both be effects of some common underlying cause, but there is certainly a close relationship between them.

I have looked on with shock and sadness as some of my friends, many of whom I have known for a great many years, find themselves with their feet to the fire, hanging out with their old cronies, talking about "the good old days." They do not want to go anywhere new, or do anything new. In some cases, of course, they do not want to go anywhere or do anything, but at least they do not want to go to a restaurant to which they have not gone before; they do not want to eat any new foods; they do not want to meet any new people; and they most positively do not want to encounter any new idea!

This is what it means to grow old, and I do not know if it causes the deterioration of the physical body, or if it is the other way around: that the waning of physical vitality of the body causes the spirit to wither as well. Nor is it necessary for these two trends to advance at the same rate; in many cases, the trends completely diverge. Plenty of people suffer some degree of physical impairment, accident, or ill health without giving in to the deterioration of their life spirit as well, retaining an interest in life, learning new things constantly, and always open to new ideas.

All of my life I have been very strongly attracted to young people, and I have finally been able to put into words why that is. According to my understanding of metaphysics, this Quest for Novelty, the reaching Out from the Center, is one of the two aspects of God (as just one of any number of expressions which represent the same idea, Tao, for example), both of them of equal importance. The other aspect of God is the movement In towards the Center.

It is no coincidence that I have expressed the same idea before: it is the only idea there is (relating to the Second Arcanum, that is). I have also tried to emphasize, at every opportunity, the equal importance of both directions. The movement out and away from the center starts off as Novelty, Creativity, and Complexity, but, if it continues without returning to the Center, it goes off towards Error, Confusion, and Chaos.

In fact, the path of spiritual advancement is exactly this convergence back at that point of Origin, where all good things come together in

Perfection, Clarity, Balance, Harmony, Peace, Joy, Health, and Love. The process towards that goal is described by the Hermetic Alchemists as the alternation between SOLVE ET COAGULA, "to separate, and to unite" – the alternation between movement outward and movement inward.

Completum est quod dixi de Operatione Solis.

Money, Power, Politics, & God

April, 2013

It is clear to everyone that there is something terribly wrong with our world today, but no one seems to know just exactly what the problem is, or what to do about it. The financial markets seem to be central to it all, and, in fact, it boils down to Money as the root and center of the problem, which will come as a big surprise to everyone.

Historically, the history of civilization has mainly been a non-stop game of King of the Mountain, based on the simple principle that superior force will win the point. That game is still going on, and it isn't going to go away any time soon, but there is an aspect of Power that has become more and more important lately. The consequences of physical war at today's level of capability of destruction would mean the end of life on earth, or at least the end of human life. There may be breeds of insects that will be able to adapt and survive, but the human race is finished, about the time that the planet is totally worn out, anyway. No, in today's world, Money is the dominant expression of Power, and it is intimately connected to all other problems; it just depends upon the point of view.

When you understand the meanings of the Colors of the Aura, you will begin to see them easily (*vide: Tetragrammaton* and *The Colors of the Aura*). On this scale, the Planet Earth, *Gaia*, is struggling at the limits of survival, way down at the Reds and Violets. Only Black is lower down, as the absence of all life.

I think there may have been a time, perhaps not much more than 500 years ago, when the Earth was a green and healthy planet, very much a going concern, glowing bright Yellow and Green, with some very bright flashes of White Light. And now look at it! It is barely alive at all, and struggling on a daily basis for survival. There are plenty of human beings who have been there, let alone planets.

It is true that the Modern Age has seen some incredible developments: the whole Computer and Internet Age has sprung up from nowhere, establishing a very certain line in the history of the evolution of the human race. Yet, at the same time, the biological side of the picture has been bleak to unsustainable. The Earth is dying; and this is a problem the human race will just have to solve, because if the planet no longer supports life, nothing else is worth very much.

But, even though some observers try to demonstrate practical ways in which the ravages of this decline might be abated, it almost seems to have been given up as a lost cause, and everyone simply grabs what they can as they prepare to jump ship. But it is like the sinking of the Titanic, where there really wasn't anywhere the passengers could safely go, so they died.

This biological problem with the planet is not the only threat to the survival of the human race: at the same time there is monumental confusion about the role of money and banking, and the world is embroiled in endless political skirmishes as people struggle for survival or dominance in one place or another. All three of these problems come together, and they have to be solved all at once and together, and from the beginning, *ex cathedra*.

The solution to Political chaos is perfectly obvious: of course there must be one world government; that goes without saying. Visionaries like Teilhard de Chardin, Bertrand Russell, H. G. Wells, and Einstein have known it all the time. It is obvious and inescapable.

But it is the Money problem that I want to address directly here. "Money" is a universal abstraction, like Time, and Power. You cannot say, "We have agreed not to observe Time anymore; for us, time no longer exists." Nor can you say, "We have all agreed not to observe Power anymore, and we have all turned in our guns." Neither can you do away with the concept of Money. You cannot reject Money without rejecting Mathematics, which, as everyone knows these days, is the basis of the Origin of the Cosmos, or God (Pythagorean school).

It was simple enough to figure out the solution to the problem of Power: there must be a single, one world government. But the solution to the enigmas of Money are far more complex, and many attempts have been made to explain how it all works.

But, since we decide to begin at the top, *ex cathedra*, the present historical chaos of financial entanglements is all wrong in so many ways! Most people have begun to realize by now that the entire "banking industry" is a fraud, designed to perpetuate the wealth of the owners above everyone else. There is no reason why "money" has to imply any debt to anyone, certainly not the banks, which are the beneficiaries of the whole program. So, of course, we must start with a *tabula rasa,* so that we might be uncluttered with historical baggage. The first conclusion is that there must only be one Currency. That's not an exclusive demand: no other money! The point is that there must be One final medium of Exchange, against which anything else may be measured (the annual tax on property, for example). This Original Central Bank will be in the care of a very carefully selected Trustee. My own idea is to entrust the responsibility of selection to a Seminary of students drawn from all over the world at an early age to form a School of International Studies, which would self-select one of themselves to represent them as the Trustee. But other selection methods might be suggested.

Since Money is a universal abstraction, an examination into the workings of financial transactions will provide a very complete picture of all energy in the system. The Human Race, and all of *Gaia*, is currently enjoying the historical inheritance of Money/Power, playing itself out on the stage of the world. A jungle of private banks and corporations is like a jungle of sovereign states, or a jungle of wild animals, or a jungle of hungry men. There must be One World, *Gaia*; One Currency of Exchange; and One Primary Bank, under the direction of a Trustee of the World who has been very carefully chosen.

The operation of money becomes very simple: the Trustee of the World would maintain a Currency for the settlement of transactions; and they would set rates of exchange at their discretion. The One Bank would create the Currency at will, and regulate its growth and supply by a tax on property, whenever the money supply exceeded levels determined to be optimum. The Trustee would be the Director of this Bank.

Since the World Bank would have unlimited funds, it would simply spend the money in ways that would seem to maximize the effectiveness or necessity of what it needs to do. For example, my idea of providing free farms where anyone can go and simply eat and sleep for free, could be maintained at no cost whatsoever: to a very large extent, the State will want to put plenty of Money out into the world, and this is an excellent way to do it! Of course, spending money to feed hungry people, or building hospitals and schools and roads, will always be useful. Now, all action decisions are based on the profit motive, which is a very big mistake. At the level of global survival, it is an entirely unacceptable process. Yes, a gradual increase of the supply of money can go on forever, but when it exceeds its optimal expansion, it is possible to reel it back in through a universal property tax. (No other taxes would need to be applied, other than a "resource depletion tax" which would be levied specifically to regulate consumption, not to reduce the money supply.)

I think that the important place to begin is to assemble a Seminary of Candidates, carefully selected from all over the world, for expressions of potential excellence. I would like to find a benefactor who would cover the expenses of founding such an institution. An International School of International Studies, in which every candidate is accepted at full scholarship for life, would certainly create a very powerful ferment.

This is an Alchemical Vessel, and the ferment that would result could very well be considerable and could produce the energies required for the accomplishment of the Great Work of Alchemy, and an Incarnation of God on Earth, Who will own the Bank, and spend the Money.

Finally, whence comes the final authority for this Trustee? Of course, it can only come from God. There seem to be very few people left on our planet, as it is worn down to a sorry frazzle, who know how to get strength from God anymore.

I am presupposing that the final selection of the Seminary of the World as Trustee will not only produce someone who will be extremely competent and will fulfill the expectations people will have, but who will also become the channel for a very huge jolt of energy, which will seem to be a manifestation of God, *Theophany*. Actually, the energy behind this is God, and this is a deliberate exercise of classical magic.

The world needs a new Avatar. None of the others have really satisfied all requirements, although some of them have enjoyed an extended vogue, at times. The concept of the Divine Right of Kings comes from the obvious idea that the power of a King can only come from God. There is no other way this can work.

All we have to do is set it in motion by selecting a Seminary of Candidates for Trustee of the World. The school itself will set up its own energy and momentum, and participate in the unfolding of the infinite cosmos.

When the Trustee has been selected, it will be up to Him or Her to achieve the recognition and acceptance required to ride to a position of closure, when everything is settled to the point where the Trustee is regarded more and more widely as the central authority and final bank for the settlement of transactions worldwide. Money means Credit, and the intention is to settle that in one place, to establish a solid base upon which the foundations for the future evolutions of the human race can be established.

The Interim of Transition may provide unimaginable obstacles. But if it succeeds, then World Peace would be achieved, and a new Golden Age will supervene.

The Colors of the Aura

2013 – 2017

When you add the Colors of the Aura to the patterns of energy described by the trigrams of the *I Ching*, the planets of Astrology, and the metals of Alchemy, it is easy to see anything in terms of its life energy just by considering the visual impact represented by the color of its aura. When Life is broken down into its elements, there is Chaos and Death at the bottom, then Aggression and Failure, War and Peace, the Giving and Receiving of Love, and, at the top, the Point of Perfection, Love, and Bliss: Union with God.

There are eight patterns of energy in this cycle of life, and each one can be easily understood by means of its color: Black is the color of death and chaos; Red is aggression and anger; Purple is rejection and defeat; Orange is war; Blue is peace; Yellow is giving love; Green is receiving love; and White is union with God.

The color of the aura reflects the spiritual evolution or consciousness of the energy form. These auras are not only visible in people, but plants and animals, and even planets, may be seen with their auras clearly visible. There is a simple and obvious hierarchy of spiritual evolution, from the violence and anger of the lower levels, to the higher and much healthier expressions of life energies reaching upwards to love and union.

The theory of alchemy is that the process of change follows an underlying pattern that can be seen in everything that happens. The progression through the metals, from Lead to Gold, has been understood as an analogy to the progress of the soul or consciousness of man, as expressed in the color of his aura. In an earlier article *(The Metaphysics of Sex)*, these same patterns of energy were viewed within the context of sexual expression.

At the end of life, back to the original chaos, there is the color Black. Then there are the edges of life and death: Red, the color of aggression, anger, and violence, and Purple, the color of oppression, rejection, and failure. Above this there are the energies represented by the colors Orange and Blue: war and peace. From here, the ranks thin out considerably, as so much of the world, its animals, its plants, and its people, seem to be living their lives in the realms of the lower energies, represented by the darker colors of their aura. Planet Earth, Gaia, is dying, twisting and turning in the sordid colors of Red, aggression, anger, and violence, and the Purple of oppression, rejection, and defeat, always edged with Black, and within all of this turmoil on the face of the planet, most of the plants, animals, and people living on the earth seem to be affected by that powerful vortex of negative energy, and so they are caught up in the same energies and colors.

In fact, a considerable amount of energy has to be expended in order to get some upward traction in spiritual evolution, in the face of a dying planet that no longer supports life. There have been many efforts to turn this around, first on a personal level, and then on a planetary level, but the heavy weight of inertia makes it hard to break free. So it is perfectly clear: if we want our world to survive, and to grow into a healthier world for us to live in, it is essential for all animals, plants, and people to elevate the horizons of their spiritual growth, so that, as Gaia, we can continue to survive.

Voltaire figured out long ago that we should all go out and work in the garden: that is the solution to all of the problems of the world. All systems of life must follow the natural process, from organic composting, mulch, and earth worms, to a complete avoidance of chemical fertilizers for the fields, and pharmaceutical drugs for people and animals. These drugs are all of a piece, and they are killing off the bees, and soon the genetically modified soybean and corn, along with copious amounts of glyphosate Round-Up, will kill off the rest of us. It is already happening: the growing prevalence of cancer is just one of the visible effects of living in a world environment which is becoming more and more toxic to life.

So, let us go out and work in the garden, and, with enough sunshine and rain, there will be plenty of green once again on the earth. All of our wounds have to heal, and we must all together try to ascend to a healthier state of Life, and try to nurture our planet and ourselves back to health.

●

BLACK

☷ K'un

Solitude or Death

The Priest – The Magician – The Madman

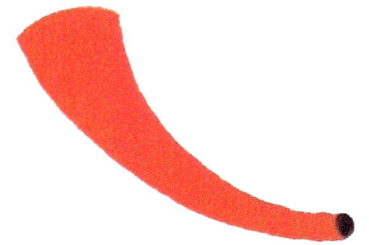

RED

☳ Chên

Aggression, Anger, or Violence

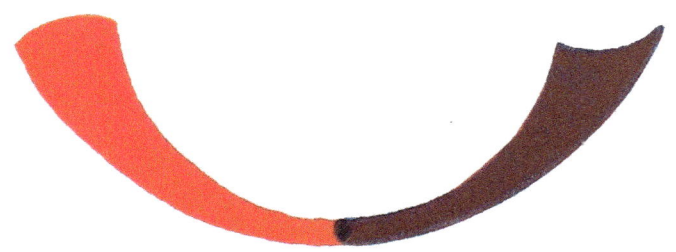

PURPLE

☷ Kên

Oppression or Suffering

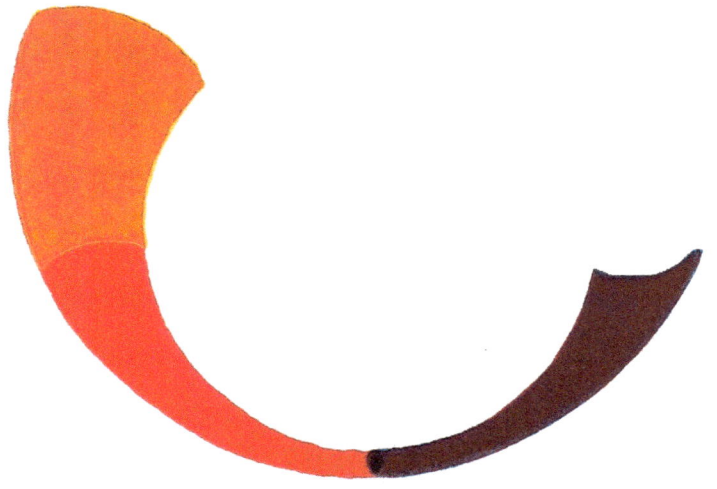

ORANGE

☲ Li

Conflict, War

BLUE

☵ K'an

Peace

YELLOW

☱ Tui

Giving Love

GREEN

☴ Sun

Receiving Love

WHITE

☰ Ch'ien

Union with God

.

COAGULA

GIVE	Gold	RECEIVE
Tin	Sun	Copper
Jupiter	Creative	Venus
Joyous	Heaven	Gentle
Lake	Ch'ien	Wind, Wood
Tui		Sun

CONFLICT — Quicksilver, Mercury, Clinging, Fire, Li

Kan, Water, Abysmal, Moon, Silver — PEACE

Chên, Thunder, Arousing, Mars, Iron — EXPAND

Kun, Earth, Receptive, Earth, Prima Materia

Kên, Mountain, Keeping Still, Saturn, Lead — CONTRACT

SOLVE

Priests and Pedophiles

May, 2013

Now it is March of 2013, and the Pope has resigned, and Francis has been elected Pope of the Catholic Church. While I have not yet noticed that anyone has made a direct connection between the resignation of the Pope and the pedophile priest problem which has overwhelmed the once-proud Catholic Church, it appears fairly evident that it is a case of a CEO taking the fall when some serious impropriety happens under his watch.

It is almost hard to imagine the Church soldiering on, in the face of such astonishing stories, not just astonishing in themselves, but because there are so many of them. Along the way, blame is attached to senior bishops and cardinals who seemed to have known about the problem without taking any significant steps. So, finally, the Pope has resigned, effectively admitting that his own negligence had been at fault in the matter: the Pope is the one who is responsible for the Church.

But, is the resignation of the Pope enough to salvage the Catholic Church from terminal opprobrium? Trying to reconcile this very large religious body, which pretends to offer ministry and services in the name of Jesus Christ (who famously loved children too, of course), with such an extensive history of pedophile priests seems to be impossible. What can it all mean, and what kind of lessons can we, as a human race, learn from this experience?

Are all these priests, for example, simply wolves in priest's clothing, pretending to be walking with God, while they are secretly only interested in advancing the fulfillment of their own lusts? I do not think that that is a useful way to look at what has been going on. If there were only a few isolated incidents, we might take the view that those "priests" involved were simply vicious criminals fraudulently hiding under their clerical collars. But the reported incidents are just too widespread and numerous, and found in every corner of the world; to imagine that all of these persons are just monsters in league with the Devil seems to me to be an inadequate interpretation. I want to look further and deeper to discover what has really been going on.

In the first place, there is the question of celibacy, which is central to the whole issue. Celibacy is clear and obvious, and even almost essential in a religious context. In other words, a person who is celibate will operate from a state which is unlike the normal experience of people who interact with each other. Even when interactions between people are not specifically sexual, there is the same underlying dynamic going on.

To a very large extent, there is a whirlwind of energy which carries the massive energy flow of the human race, as it continues its evolutionary unfolding into its infinite and unknown future. All of life, all human beings, even all plants and animals on this earth, are caught up in this massive energy flow. All of the infinite comedy of the human race unfolds from the unwinding of this endless cord. But a priest, who is not connected to the energy stream sexually, is alone, and must make his peace with God, or else be thrown off in any direction out into error, madness, chaos, and finally death.

Certainly priests who have had sexual contacts with children are committing the very error for which the state of celibacy is so important. But it remains for me a meaningless question to ask if the Catholic Church should end the celibate priesthood. The state of celibacy does exist (though rarely); a person who is not celibate is missing the whole point of what it means to be a "priest." We might say that "priest" means "someone who is celibate, and does not participate in sexual interaction." The wise woman, witch, or magician was likewise always a solitary practitioner; it's part of the job description. Magicians and Priests share an important core similarity. That solitary point of view, so that you can only find balance in your life by remaining very close to God, is the essence of the priest. A magician is very similar, only he pursues the objectives of his own will, rather than attempting to participate in the furtherance of the Will of God. This is the arrogance of Satan, who wishes to take the place of God, described by John Milton in his famous epic poem, *Paradise Lost*.

Historically, the Magician who tries to implement his own agenda, apart from the Will of God, will always, sooner or later, fall off the cliff into error and madness. *The Lord of the Rings* was a great story, philosophically, in which it was understood that the only way to resolve the problem created by the *Ring of Power* was to destroy it! I found the movie to be an excellent portrayal of the story, but I regretted that cinematic necessity required the foreshortening of the role of Saruman. Saruman was originally the head of the order of wizards to which Gandalf belonged, but acquisition of greater and greater knowledge and power eventually led to his corruption and downfall; all of this was overlooked in the movie, and Saruman was reduced to the status of a simple villain. Insofar as a Magician deviates from the Will of God, he falls into error and will sooner or later be destroyed. (Words may be variously defined, but most understandings of a "magician" or "wizard" do not automatically imply opposition to the Will of God; in most cases, the wizard acquires his influence and power from his greater understanding of the complex energy fields determining the flow of events on earth.)

A "priest" who were not celibate, would be no different from a friendly neighbor; he would not be a Priest, one of the Hands of God on earth.

So I continue searching further to discover meaning in these events. One lesson which is clear is that it is not at all easy to live a life of celibacy! It is not for everyone, and no one should attempt to follow that path who is not prepared for what it means. Sex is a kind of biological necessity for most of the human race; the only way for the celibate man (or woman) to retain his balance is to stand with God; if he stands in opposition to God, he will sooner or later fall apart into madness and chaos. The celibate man has no sex with man or woman, boy or girl (or his dog or his goat), but he has "sex" with God alone. ("How do you have sex with God," the child asks, in confusion. – well, try yoga, for example.)

I find the intercourse of human relationships to be a much more simple matter than most people seem to understand, and I have sorted the matter out into a correspondence with the eight patterns of the primary trigrams of the I Ching (as well as the planets and metals of astrology and alchemy, and the colors of the aura). (*vide: Patterns of Illusion and Change*, reprinted in *The Laughter of God*). Every person has an aura color in accordance with the energy patterns they express: the Red and Violet are the colors of aggression and oppression. Orange and Blue are fire and water, war and peace. Gold and Green are giving and receiving love. White is the full state of love and union; and Black is the state of solitude or death.

So I can understand the state of Solitude, Black, as being very close to God, identical in one essential aspect with the opposite point at the union of love, which is also identical with God. (Perfect Union and complete Solitude are really the same thing, only on different levels.)

I search for the root of this problem with pedophile priests, and I find that the source of the problem is not that there is too much sex going on; the problem is that there is not enough (love)! There isn't nearly enough love in the world. Of course I understand that only a very tiny minority of "sex" has anything to do with love. I believe that love is very good, and absolutely essential for a healthy life; and children need love most of all. When sex is an expression of love, then it is Good. There are far too many people living without the support of love. From the state the world is in, I think that there are very few people truly enjoying the state of love. This is the root of a very serious problem which must be addressed if there is to be any hope at all for the survival of life on earth. (By the way, I should clarify that when I say "everyone needs love," I do not mean everyone needs to receive love, although that is also true; what I mean is that everyone has to discover the liberation and joy of giving love.)

Now I imagine that every person's energy field can be understood by analogy with the colors of the aura. Some people's lives are smoldering down among the Red, Violet, and Black aura colors, just barely alive, perhaps on the way out; other people are struggling between war and peace: Orange and Blue, all their lives long; but others are giving and receiving love:

Yellow and Green; and others (very few, and, for the most part, it is very rare and sporadic) are at the peak of love itself, radiating a White light and a powerful and loving energy field. You can easily interpret a person's level of spiritual growth from looking at their aura. The "fully self-realized yogi" (there are many names for this state: Nirvana, Samadhi. etc.) may be recognized as an avatar of God.

It is not "sex" which is bad; it is the confusions and problems which develop from the lower levels of sexual expression, due to ignorance and unresolved karma, which are the cause of troublesome consequences. If everyone were taught this simple sex-by-color dial, they could make all of their sexual intentions very clear, so there should be no problem. (– or, fewer problems: it is hard to rejoice when our love is not returned, but, at least if all of the energies are clear, then there will be fewer misunderstandings about the intentions of the relationships, and the overall sex-economic energy flow will be much less impeded by problematic frustration and stasis.)

I think everyone should learn the joy of loving other people. I want to suggest that everyone should think, not just of finding one other person to love, but one of each gender! If everyone had a "best friend" of their own gender as well as a partner of the opposite gender, that is twice as much available love going on as before. I have never considered homosexual love to be an alternative sexual arrangement, but an additional experience, presenting its own additional opportunities for loving expression. It is very much too bad that many people used to believe that a total social break had to be made in order to realize the desire for close contact with one's own gender. Fortunately, I see a growing trend away from this absurdly limiting concept towards an awareness of far more open and inclusive possibilities of loving contacts.

I even think it would be interesting for people to live in various triangular arrangements, more or less stable, as alternative domestic relationships, because of the greatly increased social dynamic involved. I have been interested in these ideas all of my life, but it seems to be very rare, and it is certainly a different topic. The Number Three is the number of Magic, and is the basis for a whole explosion of possibilities; I have written articles along these lines, most of them unpublished or obscurely published.

I think children should be encouraged to form close friendships with their chosen friends. One of the single most damaging problems affecting the evolution of the human race is that little boys (especially) are made to discover that fighting is natural and good, but love is completely forbidden. The little boy who comes home all bloody from a fight will make his father glad and proud as long as the other boy fared at least as badly. But what might happen should our schoolboy discover that he loves one of his male friends, and brings him home to meet his family? The short answer is that the little boy will very quickly learn a very important social lesson, and he will never again make the same mistake! Or, if he does continue to feel a fondness for his male friends, he will certainly hide it and deny it, with all of the karmic burden that all of that entails.

Everyone needs love, and children need love especially! I have always been attracted to children, but it is the ones who need love that especially arouse my interest. As a child, I never bonded with my mother. I grew up very much alone, socially. I needed love when I was young, but there was nowhere I could find it. I felt a huge, unfulfilled need. Now, when I see other children with that same need, my heart goes out to them. I wonder if pedophile priests feel the same way I do? Perhaps, in the course of their daily experience, they come across children who are neglected, or otherwise in need of some loving attention. A priest who is close to God will be very sensitive to children who are in need of love. We are all in need of love, but, by the time we are adult, most of us have learned how to cope with life according to the cards that are dealt out to us. Children, on the other hand, should not be left to flail about alone, without some guidance and love! Perhaps priests are loving children because there are so many children in need of love.

But that isn't the story we are hearing – we hear only of "abuse." Because of the supercharged sexual climate in which we are living (because there isn't enough loving sex going around), it is no longer possible for adults to have any friendly relations at all with children. This means that every kind of close contact will only cause problems, and recoil badly upon both child and man. (By the way, why is it that when women love children it is considered natural and good, yet when a man loves children, the only interpretation anyone can imagine is that the man is a predatory monster? Is it really so out of character for men to love children? I think, in many cases, people only see the world through their own lenses.)

As for the Catholic church, I think they should allow a "non-celibate clergy," because of all the problems associated with attempted celibacy (and because it has become increasingly difficult to find persons willing to enter the priesthood), but they should also set up a new monastic order devoted to that celibacy which seeks union with God, so that there will remain some sort of structure maintaining a celibate priesthood, an essential institution for any truly religious order. Simply stated, you can't have a "religion" without celibate priests.

But, somehow, children have to find a way to experience and share love, if there is to be any hope for the future of life on earth. I think they should expect to receive it first of all from their parents, and then from a gradually widening circle of friends, mostly close to their own age at first, and probably starting with their own gender, but expanding to include the other gender as soon as their interest inclines them in that direction. Later on there is no reason why they shouldn't develop close and loving friendships with older people too (of either gender) and adults. It is well known, for example, that "pedagogical love," in which teacher and student love each other, promotes a dramatically accelerated acquisition of knowledge; this has been demonstrated over and over, and by now enjoys the status of an incontestable truth. (Since I am not attempting to publish in the "scholarly quarterlies," I do not take the trouble to prepare footnotes, but I am sure anyone could easily do so.)

Anyone who doesn't have a regular sexual partner is at risk of finding a "socially unacceptable solution" to the biological necessity of sexual relationship. Therefore, the obvious solution is to pair them up! Sometimes I think that the Reverend Sun Myung Moon wasn't so far off in many of his ideas. I believe in World Unification, and I think pairing up more people into sexual partners is a good idea. I definitely go beyond, though: I really want to explore the idea that everyone "should" have a partner of each gender, or at least be open to that possibility. Or, sometimes a person may have two or more close and lasting domestic partners, of the same or different genders – I think that in the infinite variation of human expression, any solution which suits the participants should be considered socially acceptable. Whatever promotes more loving contacts between people is all good. It is the infinite variety of human experience which creates the potential for so many different solutions for resolving sexual and relationship issues. Perhaps, if more children were allowed to grow up in a "sex-positive" environment, they would grow and develop with more normal needs and desires, and there would be much less need for some of the more surprising variations of sexual expression. Oscar Wilde's famous epigram is actually very profound: *The only way to get rid of a temptation is to yield to it.* Yielding to a desire is far better than repressing it – in most cases, unusual desires will be abandoned after some experimentation, yet repressed desires will go on working their toxic effects for the lifetime of the individual involved, until and unless unraveled through psychiatric therapy.

So, do I think all of these priests are innocent of the charges leveled against them? Of course I have no knowledge of any specific circumstances, but there are two ideas which could make some of these incidents more understandable and less problematic: in the first place, the criminal justice system automatically defines any close, loving contact between adults and children as abusive: "the perpetrator assaults the victim." This language hijacks the actual events and does not allow for any other considerations or interpretations of the events. The second idea is that any child who has had any contact with a priest understands (or his family and friends will understand for him) that it is a very easy matter to jump onto the gravy train and reap settlements sometimes running into millions of dollars simply by lodging a complaint. This alone is quite enough to color any person's memory of a childhood contact. We add the confusion with which most children react to these contacts: they have no way of understanding these contacts apart from the prevailing context with which all of modern society immediately views them.

Finally, I would like to contribute two representatives from the countervailing literature of pedophilia, both from Holland, where, until recently with the unrelenting homogenization of social attitudes internationally, sexual contact between adults and children was not necessarily considered a serious problem, in the absence of any complaint.

The first case is the formal research study conducted in Holland by Theo Sandfort, published as *Sexual Aspects of Pedophile Relations*. The study was deliberately limited to relationships between adults and children (men and boys, in this study) which were not demonstrably abusive, in which the children were willing participants, and the friendships were not one-off contacts but ongoing relationships. The study covered about thirty such relationships, and both men and boys were extensively interviewed over a period of time. The study came up with entirely neutral results – no problems were found with any of the relationships; in some cases positive social benefits were seen, but these results were not considered statistically relevant, so no conclusions were drawn.

It is essential to understand that the reason why no problems were found was that the social environment in which these men and boys lived was fairly neutral about their affairs. When any similar relationships are discovered in almost any other country (or even contemporary Holland, whose famous tolerance has been eroded by the inexorable effects of unrelenting world-wide condemnation of any contacts between adults and children) the police are called in to intervene and the child is subjected to such a literally mind-altering experience of hysterical reaction, that the poor child, having no other alternative view ever expressed in his presence, can only conclude that he has somehow participated in some very horrible activity, for which he will be forever condemned. And if − horror compounded upon horror − the child actually enjoyed the contacts, his stinking corruption and essentially vile and worthless nature is even more blatantly etched forever in stone in his own mind as well as that of his family and friends. Again, without footnotes, I believe it has been abundantly proven that the negative consequences of criminal prosecution vastly outweigh the negative consequences, if any, of the original experiences (we are only considering consensual and loving experiences here; violent rape or any other expressions of the Red/Violet of aggression against a helpless or weaker victim are an entirely different matter, not at all the subject of the present essay, and only mentioned for contrast and clarification). In other words, the prevailing social attitudes are by far the most important determinant of how the contacts will be experienced by the persons involved, or anyone else.

The next experience I want to mention is an experimental program which was conducted in Holland many years ago. I do not have access to my original sources, but I believe I found the discussion in the book *Loving Boys*, by Dr. Edward Brongersma, who was elected to the Dutch Senate in spite of his earlier history of contact with boys. The experimental program consisted of an alternative treatment for youthful offenders (boys) − they were offered a choice of traditional incarceration in juvenile detention facilities, or placement with an adult male pedophile, who would give them love! The results were not at all surprising to me: in almost every case, the boys so placed easily evolved their patterns of behavior away from anti-social activities (fraud, theft, drug abuse, violent crime, etc.) and became happy, well-adjusted members of society, not even becoming gay, unless they were inclined that way to begin with; their sexual orientation was not affected by their experience. In contrast with these results, boys placed in juvenile detention showed a dramatically worse prognosis: they were set onto a path leading to their becoming hardened criminals and repeat offenders. However, even though the results of this brief experiment in social therapy were overwhelmingly positive, the program was cancelled, as it was just considered far too radical even for the tolerant Dutch to accept.

In earlier times, men loving boys was a very common experience: teacher/student, master/apprentice, knight/squire, etc. (going back at least to Ancient Greece, where a young man who didn't have an older male lover was at a distinct social disadvantage – the men who loved these boys, by the way, usually had normal relationships with wife and family in addition to their beloved boy companion and friend). In most cases, such alliances were looked on as advantageous for the boy, who enjoyed many benefits from the affection of his older friend; the man involved was often laughed at as "throwing away his love on a boy," but there was rarely any serious opposition; it was just another way in which the infinite workings of the human experience found to work out the sexual karma of the participants. (*vide, e.g., The Autobiography of Benvenuto Cellini,* a most remarkable book in many ways, in which boy-love was casually referred to as a relatively common experience: the apprentice who enjoyed the Master's love enjoyed special privileges and benefits; both man and boy were frequently envied for their happy affair or laughed at for their folly, but never condemned, unless there were additional problematic circumstances.)

The present day hysterical "witch-hunt" against adults who love children (again, not to be confused with a violent or aggressive Red on Purple attack against a helpless victim) is symptomatic of a sick society, most of which is itself mired in the relentless and ugly aggression and violence which is dragging our world down towards the end of life on this once-fair planet.

One problem, as I see it, is that persons who live their lives at any level of social expression, represented by the color of their aura, can only understand energies at their own level or below; they have no knowledge or understanding of the higher levels at all! That is, people whose lives are an endless round of violence and aggression believe that that is the nature of the dog-eat-dog world, and if "a fool is born every minute, every five minutes one is born to take them." The idea that there might be something better or higher totally escapes them.

As I consider the surprising revelations concerning so many thousands of priests, I just do not think that writing them all off as scoundrels and villains contributes much at all to an understanding of the problem. The problem, as I see it, is that so much of the world is experiencing the end-of-life decline into death represented by the Red and Violet aura colors, which usually ends up at Black (death), unless there is a sudden and dramatic turn-around of the collective energies of the planet.

A Modest Proposal to Achieve Peace in the Middle East

October, 2014

I write this in October of 2014, and any prospect of peace in the Middle East appears to be way beyond unlikely. The tensions between Sunni and Shia Moslems appear to be as great as the antipathy of all Moslems to the Western world or to Israel.

As I speculate upon philosophical themes as well as the obstacles to the survival of life on earth, I have come to the conclusion, shared by a great many philosophers, scholars, and visionaries of every possible kind, that the only hope for the survival of life on earth is an immediate and unprecedented evolutionary leap in global consciousness – and this really has to happen virtually overnight. The most immediate and pressing problems are ecological – the loss of the Trees, the burning off of millions of years' worth of fossil fuels in a few generations, the destruction and growing necrosis of our Oceans, the erosion of our slender resource of topsoil and the attendant cycles of severe drought and destructive flooding (all of which are directly caused by the loss of the Trees, which I have called the greatest mistake the human race has made in its relatively brief rampage of destruction upon our dear planet), the increasingly evident problems of global warming and climate change, the toxic devastation of the planet's farmland as well as our own human bodies by the incredibly stupid and myopic reliance upon pharmaceutical drugs and chemical interference with the organic patterns which have sustained the growth of human life for the many thousands of years prior to the modern era – I could go on and on, but I am not the only one beating this drum, and these issues have been raised repeatedly, although seemingly falling upon deaf ears (because it's money that makes the world go round, not love – I hate to break the news).

It's not that no one knows what to do about these problems – I have detailed a whole program of planetary restoration in a whole series of previous articles, and Lester Brown (*Plan B: World on the Edge*) has offered many excellent ideas of how the planetary slide into destruction and death can be slowed and possibly even reversed – but the problems confronting us are not primarily technological, but political and economic. I have even addressed those issues, and have come up with radical solutions which may easily be found among my writings, and need not be repeated here. I certainly do not and would not suggest that my solutions might be easily or quickly implemented, but the problems are so pressing that we must make some efforts, and do so immediately. However, my proposals for new patterns and institutions for social and economic organization, which might be made to work among the peoples of relatively stable environments, run into serious problems when faced with the rampant chaos on the ground in the Middle East. It really seems to be that an essential prerequisite to any new evolutionary growth is the radical elevation of consciousness worldwide. There is a necessary and inevitable sequence about this program of social, political, and economic institutions worldwide, and *then*, finally, we might be in a position to address the urgent program of ecological regeneration which we must tackle immediately if there is to be any hope for the survival of life on earth. Whew! Now what? I love the apocryphal image of Don Quixote "jumping on his horse and riding off rapidly in all directions," but on my last careful reading of the text, I failed to locate that passage, and I don't remember where I heard of it.

Well, not to worry – I have a solution, as usual. First, let us consider the present "conventional" approach. I think the U.S. government has racked up expenses well in excess of a trillion dollars (or multiple trillions) in fighting the "war against terror" in Iraq, Afghanistan, and now Syria. And yet, by all estimates, the world is rapidly plunging ever more deeply into chaos, and everyone is considerably less safe than they were in the year 2000.

So here is my proposal – give me just 1% of that budget, a mere $10 billion, and I will undertake to resolve all of the problems and conflicts of the Middle East within, say, ten years' time. The lions will lie down with the lambs, and everyone will beat their swords into plowshares and their spears into pruning hooks. Everyone will return happily to their farms, making love with their wives (and/or significant others), and a new Golden Age will supervene over that historically troubled land. Actually, I expect my costs to be well within one billion dollars, or even considerably less than that, but I will be happy to retain the remaining $9 billion as my fee.

By now I am sure it is clear to almost everyone how I propose to accomplish this miracle, especially to all those who realize that I am an original hippie from the 60s – of course it is obvious and very simple – we simply manufacture a few billion trips of LSD and distribute them for free all over the world. LSD, as everyone knows, has zero physical toxicity, zero addictive potential, and a high correlation with spiritual epiphany.

Sometimes I have heard of people having some bad times "with LSD," but, upon further inquiry, it *always* turns out that the person experiencing bad effects was also using some combinations of very highly toxic drugs – methamphetamines, cocaine, heroin, alcohol, sugar, etc. Those who only use LSD, with perhaps some preparation of cannabis, rarely experience any negative effects, and never are those effects physically expressed.

Of course, in order for this plan to work, it is essential that it be carried out in the West as well as the Middle East, as the need for spiritual renewal is just as pressing in the West as it is anywhere else in the world. When you take a hefty dose of LSD (usually 300-500 mcg, depending upon body weight and other factors), "you see God and you love everyone." And these two experiences describe exactly the same thing – being in the presence of God means the same thing as feeling an unlimited oceanic love for all of life – that is the spiritual epiphany.

Actually, I should clarify that the experience does not apply to the inexperienced or casual user (or someone with a low level of spiritual consciousness), and certainly not with any user who combines other drugs with the LSD experience (with the exception of moderate cannabis use, which is harmless, and anything else in very careful moderation). With most drugs, the "high" is followed by a depression which falls well below the original baseline. Each subsequent indulgence brings the experience to a less lofty high, leading ultimately to a place where the "high" is far lower than the original baseline, and the lows are the very depths of Hell. In contrast to this familiar pattern, the high of LSD is followed by a very gentle decline, but ending with a mild euphoria somewhat above the starting baseline. The physical aspects of subsequent LSD ingestion are dose dependent (somewhat modified by "set and setting"), but the spiritual high gets higher with every use, while the end state is increasingly higher, so that an occasional user might end up with an advanced spiritual consciousness as his ordinary, baseline experience. This pattern of experience has been observed numerous times, especially when the tripper's consciousness has not been negatively affected by other drugs (including excessive sugar or alcohol) or other unrelated negative experiences.

I might characterize the LSD experience as a hyper stimulation of the sensory stimuli along with an increased consciousness of the potential for novelty. It is this last characteristic that makes LSD so frightening to the conservative masters of repressive regimes. The last thing anyone in political power wants is for anyone to discover and explore the potential for novelty! Oh, no! It is no surprise that the CIA would want to control the opium crop in Afghanistan so that they could refine it into heroin and bring it to the young black men of the inner cities of New York, Los Angeles, and Chicago. They want the addict to bow his head, shuffle along, and think only about getting another fix. Can you imagine the chaos that might ensue if these oppressed minorities might open their eyes to the systematic oppression, leading (usually and deliberately) to incarceration, and instead began to consider ways of overturning the process? Such a conscious awareness could easily lead to a veritable revolution. Oh, no – keep them sedated with opiates, and then pick them off one by one and pack them off to jail.

But novelty might rear its ugly or beautiful head in a great many other ways – after a few sessions of LSD, a man might quit his job, leave his family (or bring them with him), and go off to an ashram in India in search of enlightenment. Or, he might simply quit his job selling life insurance so that he can play his alto saxophone in a jazz band. There are no limits to the potential of novelty to the expanded consciousness.

But it is only through Change that anything can get better! Now we are faced with a world that is coming apart at the seams in every way – ecologically, politically, economically, and socially. What this world needs (and, boy did it ever need it yesterday!) is a greatly augmented consciousness of the potential for change! Whether you like my own solutions to the problems of the world, or whether you prefer to follow another agenda, one thing is clear – a lot of things have got to change, and change very, very quickly if there is to be any hope for the survival of life on earth. Bring on the LSD! May the sun shine forever, and may you stay forever young.

The reason this program may take about ten years is that the rise in consciousness is neither instantaneous nor permanent – it takes a series of trips before the aspirant gradually perceives the interconnectedness and unity of all being, and begins to feel an oceanic love for all of life – plants and animals, rivers, oceans, trees, fragrant roses, and people – and, in a final epiphany, sees God in all Her Glory. Some will reach this point sooner than others (and many, of course, never reach it at all), but once a critical mass has been reached, the elevation of consciousness will become general and universal. At this point, many of the ecological changes will come about naturally as natural organic patterns of life will replace artificial and destructive ones, such as chemical fertilizers and pharmaceutical drugs. Political and economic changes will easily and quickly follow, trees will be planted everywhere (restore Paradise: dig up a parking lot), and Gaia may once again grow green and fertile, providing abundant food for everyone, and life on earth may continue.

Felix Polydactyl Meander

2015

This is an essay on gender liberation, celebrating the large and growing number of people who are neither "male" nor "female" but somewhere in between. But first I want to write about Meander, my daughter's polydactyl (many toed) cat.

When my daughter was a little girl, one of her friend's cats was having kittens. The friend offered my daughter "the pick of the litter." The kittens were born, and my daughter fell in love with one of them and happily brought it home. Now I have loved cats all my life (– and dogs and children and trees and fragrant roses), so I was happy to welcome my daughter's new kitten into our lives, but I was dismayed to discover that her choice was a polydactyl, and not just with an extra toe somewhere, but all four paws had about seven toes! It looked like he were wearing big, clumsy gloves on every paw. My daughter was so full of love and joy for her new kitten, so I muted my reaction a little bit, but I asked her why, if she were offered the pick of the litter, why she had to choose a kitten with such obvious defects. Why couldn't she have chosen a perfect kitten (none of the other kittens had any extra toes)?

But Meander (as he would later be named) was not defective at all. He was totally perfect in every way. I have known and loved a great many cats in my life, and never have I known a nicer cat. He was sweet, gentle, friendly, loving, mellow, and totally delightful. Whenever I would put on some classical music (say, a Telemann oboe concerto), Meander would come running to sit on my lap or on the end of the bed and listen to the music with me, his ears always moving to tune in the music just right. (I have always been envious of cats' ears.)

In earlier times, some people were so barbaric as to cut off the extra toes from a polydactyl, so that the cat would conform to the norm and be "just like everybody else." I don't know if my daughter selected her kitten because of the extra toes, but they certainly didn't bother her at all. My daughter was very young at the time, and I suspect that she just tuned into her kitten completely oblivious to the extra toes. I would have missed my chance – I would have been prejudiced with the attitude that I should choose a "perfect" cat, and so would have missed the joy and delight of having such a wonderful cat entering into our lives, enriching us immeasurably.

So I am sure the lesson is clear by now – you don't have to cut off any extra toes. 1000 years ago the differentiations of people into two opposite genders was much more pronounced than in the present day. All throughout history there have always been both men and women who have not conformed to this differentiation, but, for the most part, men were raised to be strong, aggressive, and warlike. War, in fact, has always been considered to be the defining occupation of a man. Women, on the other hand, were softer and nurturing – homemakers and mothers of children. But the world has changed a lot over the years, and there is less and less reason all the time for any essential polarity between men and women.

This transition has been happening gradually. In the not too distant past, fathers who considered their boys to be too soft (not to say "effeminate") might send them off to a military academy to turn them into "real men." Today's young men are increasingly rejecting that solution, but they often seem to be turning to another option which seems to me to be just as surprising – not wanting to be turned into a "real man," they sometimes try to turn themselves into "real women." Both options seem crazy to me.

Of course I hasten to proclaim my belief in the natural right to the freedom for everyone to live their life any way they please, in any way that seems good to them (and their partners), regardless of anyone's preconceived ideas of what is "right" or "natural," but, in the present essay, I want to speak up for a third option – to accept yourself exactly as you are, and to live your life just the way you want to live. You don't have to be either male or female – you can live your life happily as an in-between. You might be androgynous, or you might have some combination of male and/or female qualities. And – a lot of us like you that way! A typical aggressive male with no redeeming female virtues is an unpleasant character, in my eyes.

I remember (many years ago – the 60s) at the **Stud**, a famous gay bar in San Francisco, South of Market, you might find an astonishing assortment of faeries, twinks, drag queens, and an extravagantly costumed array of persons of indeterminate and irrelevant gender. All persons were uniquely themselves, "doing their own thing," and no two were alike, but long hair and bright colors were typical. This extraordinary, glorious, and refreshing celebration of individual freedom delighted me much, much more than the later evolution to costumed uniformity known as "the Castro

Clone" (After Castro Street, not Fidel) – short hair, lumberjack shirt, boots, mustache, and scarf around the neck or in the back pocket.

My favorite image retained from those days was of a man dancing divinely at the **Stud** in a long, flowing black gown. He wasn't trying to be a woman – he had long hair, but he also had a full beard, and he had no fake tits or painted lips or nails; he was just blazing brightly as 100% himself, whether you liked it or not. The thing is – a lot of people liked it. Just as my daughter, given the chance to take the pick of the litter, fell in love with Meander, gloves and all, so, in the same way, many people today are not looking for a "typical" or "standard paradigm" male or female, but, given the choice, we might look for someone who is somewhere in-between.

Certainly there are plenty of men, women, and in-betweens who lust after big, beefy aggressive males with a dominance personality disorder, and, in celebration of diversity, I am glad that there is someone for everyone, but I know I am not the only man who greatly prefers an "in-between male" – sweet and gentle, soft-bodied, somewhat feminine – an artist or musician rather than a football player. I have always been entirely bisexual, and I have loved women all my life, but I have always preferred tough, independent women with flat chests and narrow "boyish" hips to the apparently more popular big-breasted bimbos. But I am most highly aroused by sweet, gentle, and pretty young men of low testosterone, who are more likely to be found baking bread than playing football or joining the army.

So, to all the lovely young men who fit my phantasy profile, please don't join any army in hopes of being turned into a "real man" – but you don't have to turn yourself into a woman, or cut off any toes, either – I love you just the way you are, and I'm not the only one.

Not Enough Love in the World

August, 2016

I worry a lot about the state of the world; there are so many things going wrong that the planet isn't going to last long at the present rate of the loss of vitality. "Gaia" is dying, and everything from wars to droughts are caused by the declining vitality of the planet. Taken as a whole, the planet shows a fairly low level of spiritual consciousness. I try to look for the root cause of the problem – fear, poverty, oppression – and it all comes down to the same thing. In order for planetary consciousness to rise, it is necessary for the consciousness of individual people to rise. I have described eight patterns of consciousness in my writings (*vide, e.g., Patterns of Illusion and Change,* reprinted in *The Laughter of God),* but the main axis goes from infinite clarity, love, and joy, to deepening confusion, anger, violence, chaos, and death.

The overall level of planetary consciousness is way too low, down in the struggle for survival in the Red and Violet range. Most of the world is barely above that in the range of Orange and Blue – war and peace. How can we raise the level higher, to regions of expanding love? I have several suggestions:

In the first place, everyone would benefit from a clearer understanding of these spiritual levels. Since every aspect of one's life improves as one rises in spiritual consciousness, this should create a self-reinforcing process of growth, depending upon how clearly the process be understood. But, instead of waiting for a slowly elevating spiritual consciousness to raise the amount of love in the world, it is also possible for increasing amounts of love in the world to accelerate the growth in spiritual consciousness.

One way to accomplish this objective is to broaden the scope of loving contacts. For most people, "love" means the perfect union at the top of the diagram, the color White (*vide: Tetragrammaton*). But circumstances are not always right for the expression of this pattern. However, the Green and Gold, right below the White, offer alternative possibilities of loving contact – giving and receiving love. In this case, the receiving party is relatively passive. The reciprocal love represented by the color White is the pinnacle of spiritual consciousness, but is not always an available choice. Expressions in the Gold and Green range are far more easily accessible.

Another idea for propagating larger amounts of love may seem pretty radical, but it could accomplish an even doubling of the available love in the world if the policy were adopted. There are two primary genders of people in the world, with a great many variations of expression in between, but it has always surprised me that everyone seems to be expected to confine their sexual interest to only one of the genders. Even in the case of gay (or otherwise queer) persons, it is usually expected that all of one's contacts will be of one gender or the other. But what a different world it would be if the normal expectation of everyone were not to find any one perfect (or otherwise) partner, but to find one partner (or best friend) of each gender! You do the math – it amounts to a neat doubling of available love in the world. It makes sense to me. There are (at least) two genders out there, and they are generally quite different in many ways, but *I like them both* (I also like most of the alternative genders, while we are at it, especially those in between the extremes of male or female expression). I have a normal interest in women, and the kinds of relationship possible with women, but I also have an equal, if different, interest in men, and the kinds of relationship possible with men.

This idea leads naturally to my next idea – if men and women are going to be loving more than one gender, it becomes possible to consider a larger scope of domestic establishment. In fact, the possibilities of domestic establishment exactly parallel the sequence of the primary mysteries of nature or philosophy (*vide: Tetragrammaton*). The first possibility (corresponding to the First Arcanum) is Solitude.

A person who is altogether alone has no center, or ground of being, except as noted below. There are three common manifestations of this pattern – the Priest, the Magician, and the Madman. The Madman, of course, has lost all touch with reality, and all of the elements of his life spin off into confusion and chaos.

The Priest centers his life around the Will of God. The questions about a celibate clergy are meaningless, as celibacy is practically the definition of a priest. The Magician, on the other hand, knows only his own will. The exercise of a personal will, while practically the definition of life itself, is fraught with danger. While the Magician tries to protect himself within magic circles, the danger to the Magician is not so much the presence of evil spirits which might penetrate his magic circle, as it is that the energies he unleashes in the furtherance of his own will will turn back upon himself to his own destruction.

The Pair Bond is the primary unit of human relationship known most famously as the union of Male and Female, and representing the Second Arcanum of metaphysics. There are a great many variations on this theme; in the first place, the male and female energies do not necessarily have to be represented by biologically male and female genders, nor do both parties have to be human, or even alive – for example, a man and his dog, or a junkie with his "wife" (his syringe outfit – but this "pair bond" is a very thinly disguised example of solitude, in the aspect of madness).

Furthermore, pairings of two male energies, or two female energies (again, not necessarily represented by the nominal gender) are often found, though not nearly as frequently as the paradigm male and female.

But if all that sounds complicated, the endless novelty of Triangles, involving an intentional relationship of three persons, goes way beyond. The dynamics of a Triangle are totally different from those of the Pair Bond, giving rise to an explosive multitude of social possibilities of endless complexity. This infinite unfolding of endless possibility is characteristic of the Third Arcanum.

Intentional complex relationships beyond the Triangle are also possible – patterns of Four (usually essentially two couples – the Fourth Arcanum) are probably more common than Triangles, and become the square building blocks for a stable foundation of society. A pattern of Five (the Fifth Arcanum) will exhibit many of the radical aspects of Triangles, due to the increased propensity for novelty and change, as compared with patterns of Two or Four. Communities larger than five experience diminishing returns, as the bonds grow weaker with larger numbers.

Yet another opportunity of increasing the amount of available love in the world is by the education of the young. What a radically different world this would be if parents were to teach little boys (especially) to love one another instead of fighting all the time! Children are never too young to learn about the different levels of spiritual consciousness and expression, and they can be led to the higher paths just as easily as be allowed to experience the lower levels. As a new generation of these children grow up, there will be no more war, and perhaps we could finally get to work to solve some of the pressing environmental problems that threaten the survival of life on earth.

A New Therapeutic Approach
to Deviant or Criminal Behavior

December, 2016

My thesis is very simple – it is that what I may call "spiritual consciousness" can be ranked in a clear progression through the familiar patterns represented by the Seven Planets of Classical Astrology, the Seven Metals of Alchemy, the Colors of the Aura, or the Eight Primary Trigrams of the *I Ching* (*quod vide: Tetragrammaton*). The reason Western symbolism only has seven positions instead of the eight of the trigrams is that they do not include the Earth among the planets, or include the *Prima Materia*, which is not really one of the metals. In terms of human relationship, this represents Solitude, which, properly speaking, is not really a "relationship" at all. In the same way, it is not included in the rankings of spiritual consciousness.

Referring to the ranked relationships by color, for clarity and simplicity, the lowest level is Red. Red refers to an expression of Violence or Anger, lashing out against his victim (Violet). Violet is the color of Oppression and Pain, the victim of an assault by the energy of the color Red.

The next higher level is Orange, Conflict, expressed either as individual fighting or large scale war. Above that is Blue, Peace. The higher levels of spiritual consciousness above Blue are Yellow, Giving Love; Green, Receiving Love; and, finally, at the top, is White or Union, at the highest level of which is Cosmic Consciousness and Union with God.

But what of Black, which refers to Solitude or Death, depending upon your frame of reference? As detailed in *Not Enough Love in the World*, there are three ways it can go, other than by evolving away from solitude – the Priest, the Magician, or the deepening confusion of the Madman. It is this last state that engenders most of the etiology of deviance of all kinds.

So, while this state is outside of the ranking of the spiritual consciousness of human relationships, it is the principle breeding ground of deviant or criminal behavior.

The most effective therapeutic protocol is obvious – clearly, anyone who has spent too much time alone, unless he has found God and has centered his life around fulfilling the Will of God, will either be exclusively self-centered, or he will be bouncing along randomly in confusion or chaos like a loose cannon on the deck of a ship. Hence, the most effective therapeutic protocol will be to assist in the evolution away from solitude to some variation of a pair bond.

As soon as the subject makes a biological connection with the community of human life, the elements of confusion will begin to be re-oriented around a center of life. There will still remain the evolution through the rankings of human relationship (known in alchemy as the transmutation of lead into gold). If the subject re-enters the range of the Seven Planets and Seven Metals at least as high as the Blue (Peace), it should be possible, with guidance, to evolve into the upper levels of spiritual consciousness. If, on the other hand, the subject breaks out of the Black into the Red zone, continued supervision will be recommended.

The Evolution of Theology

2016

In my own life, my ideas of religion and theology have passed through a very surprising evolution. Born the son and grandson of Methodist ministers, with my father also a PhD in Philosophy, I was familiar with religious ideas from my earliest years, dutifully attending Sunday School and Church services every week. However, being an intelligent child with an inquiring mind, I was naturally an atheist from at least the age of seven or eight. I suppose it is possible that in my yet earlier and more tender years I may have believed, or at least accepted, my father's explanations of theological questions, but as soon as I was old enough to understand the ideas which I was expected to believe, I thoroughly rejected them. "Just Who does he think is listening to those prayers he makes in church every Sunday morning?" I was embarrassed for my naive and simple-minded father, who had done so well academically, but seemed to be so lacking in mature judgment and critical discernment.

As I grew into adolescence and beyond, my rejection of all fanciful ideas of religion only hardened into a confirmed atheism. However, I found myself confronted with metaphysical questions which I could not answer. Even in my earliest days of rejection of religious answers to the primary questions of philosophy and metaphysics, I had sense enough to realize that it was not sufficient to proclaim negation; if I were going to reject the religious answers to these questions, I must put forward some credible alternatives which I could believe. In other words, to present the problem in terms of the eight-year-old atheist, if the universe were not created by God, where did it come from? (Or, "Who made God, or where did He come from?") These questions boggled my little brain, but every time I had to endure the embarrassment of listening to my father's Sunday morning prayers, I renewed my determination to understand these questions "without the use of theological postulates." Accordingly, I have spent most of my life searching for answers to these questions. I studied every source of philosophy and religion – Christian, Hebrew, Moslem, Hindu, Buddhist, Taoist, Hermetic philosophy, occult philosophy, Freemasonry, even Satanism, as well as the whole gamut of Western philosophy from Heraclitus, Pythagoras, and Plato to Wittgenstein and Whitehead.

From what started out as a huge chaos and confusion of contradictory ideas, I gradually began to discover some promising threads, finding links of remarkable similarity from widely disparate sources. The alchemical ideas of Hermetic philosophy were some of the first to impress me the most favorably. I began to see some patterns emerging out of the labyrinth of ideas, and I gradually began to understand a principle which seemed to be at the heart of the process of change. I liked the concept of the Philosophers' Stone, and thought I understood the pivotal role it played in the process of Change which lay at the heart of the mysteries. The Greeks were barking up the wrong tree looking for some fundamental particle or "atom" which was the ultimate basis of the universe. Actually, Heraclitus was onto the right approach, declaring that Change was the ultimate reality.

Gradually I developed an understanding of a whole abstract metaphysics which seemed to bring me closer and closer to an understanding of the primary mysteries of nature (referred to as the Arcana in the old mystery schools). At one point it occurred to me that I might even refer to the Philosophers' Stone as "God," and I thought that was pretty clever, to use the name of God to explain the ordering principle of my system of abstract metaphysics. Then, finally, it dawned on me that I had just discovered what many people had meant by "God" all along! But, of course, my own understanding of "God" was entirely abstract and had nothing whatever to do with that funny Being to Whom my father was addressing his prayers!

In this essay, I want to go over all of this ground again, describing how my understanding gradually evolved to a deeper understanding of the nature of God, reaching such astonishing conclusions as an understanding of the three Persons of the Trinity, and even an understanding of a personal God Who might even hear and answer prayer! And – most astonishing of all – if anyone had ever told my eight-year-old self that I would someday come to recognize Jesus Christ as the most important religious figure of all time, I would not have believed it.

Not that all of my conclusions are entirely orthodox, by any means! I have finally achieved my childhood quest of understanding the creation of the cosmos *ex nihilo,* and I have even solved the difficulty of the Problem of Evil ("How can we believe in a good, just, and merciful God when there are mosquitoes in the world?" – one of many ways in which this old problem can be expressed.) Along the way, I have come to have a radical understanding of God which is contrary to every previous conception of His nature, but which resolves all of the problems pertaining to our understanding of God. It is this new interpretation of the mystery of God which I wish to introduce in the present essay.

I wish to carry the evolution of God forward in the same sequence in which it has come to me, beginning with rejection and atheism, evolving thence into an abstract metaphysics, then emerging as a conscious and personal God, and finally revealing the outstanding importance of Jesus Christ.

Rejection and atheism is easy. It has always been easier for big sister Lucy to knock over little brother's house of blocks, laughing, than it ever was for Linus to construct his creative work of architecture in the first place.

"Where does the sky end?" was my earliest problem. It was useless for my father to assure me that the sky goes on forever – how can that be? Infinity is not a concept that an eight-year-old mind can grasp. But the infinity of time is even more puzzling than that of space. It is bad enough to assert that the universe will go on forever, but to go into the past and pretend that it has always existed is patently absurd, as any bright eight-year-old could easily assure you.

Another absurdity is the notion that we should accept the truth of revealed religion on faith! As Bertrand Russell has observed (quoted from memory, not a direct quote), "There are many hundreds of different religions in the world, all of them mutually exclusive and contradictory, so that it stands to reason, as a matter of logic, that no more than one of them could represent the truth, and all the rest of them are just bunk, so why should anyone believe that the religion into which they happen to have been born is the truth? It is more logical to assume that all of them are bunk." -- Bertrand Russell, *Why I Am Not a Christian.* I fully understand the difficulty – since it is considered to be impossible to come to any clear theological understanding by reason alone, the only recourse left to us is to accept our revealed beliefs on faith.

Well, I am here to pick two holes in that analysis. In the first place, as I researched every imaginable source of religious and philosophical ideas, I began to see many of the most important ideas cropping up again and again, clothed, it is true, in an extravagant variety of costumes, but of which certain core ideas kept coming up unmistakably again and again with surprising similarity. Eventually I began to distinguish these ideas and sort them out into a system according to their patterns. Suddenly Bertrand Russell's whole argument flipped onto its head – if the same fundamental ideas keep coming up again and again no matter how widely diverse the sources, there must be something to it!

The second hole in the idea that belief can only be based on faith since there is no way to derive an understanding of religion by reason alone is that I have done just exactly that – without relying upon faith at all – in fact, starting from a total rejection of everything I was expected to believe on faith – I have derived an understanding of metaphysics and theology which I am not only convinced is correct, but which I believe is the only solution possible to the major problems of philosophy. But what ended up as a complete and integrated system of metaphysics started out as just a series of related ideas.

One of my epiphanies along the way was to see that these ideas were most effectively illustrated by the numbers of mathematics. I understood that this was the meaning of the claim by Pythagoras that Numbers were the

Secret Key to an understanding of the Mysteries of Nature. (So, actually, this epiphany occurred to Pythagoras first, but it was an original idea to me.) "Mathematics is the language of God." The concept of Number is the mother of all abstraction. The whole field of mathematics is *a priori* knowledge that can be conceived without any reference to the external world. There is a mystery associated with the number One, another mystery associated with the number Two, another mystery associated with the number Three, and another mystery associated with the number Four. The mysteries continue, but these first four are the most important and primary. In fact, the smaller the number, the more important the mystery in a kind of logarithmic scale in which each number is more important than the one which follows. This sequence of the first four primary mysteries comprise what Pythagoras referred to as the *Tetractys*. It is represented also by the four letters of the Name of God in Hebrew (the *Tetragrammaton*).

I have written about these mysteries all of my life, from my earliest book, *Symposium by God and the Devil,* and the *Lapis Philosophorum* (I especially prefer the third edition), to the very elaborate *Theophany,* which I printed by letterpress from hand-set type on paper made by hand, to the *Patterns of Illusion and Change,* and, most recently, *Tetragrammaton,* a small book of pictures illustrating the primary mysteries, "the Keys to the Arcana." In the first two books mentioned, I presented the sequence of Arcana horizontally, one to a page. Then, in a truly major epiphany (assisted, as I recall, by the fortuitous stimulus of LSD, which enjoys a well-documented history of association with divine inspiration), I stacked the symbols vertically, and saw, to my astonishment, that I had recreated the Tree of Life from the Kabbalah! At first I thought it were just an amazing coincidence, but as I looked more closely, I saw that every sphere on the Tree of Life corresponded exactly to its relative position on my own diagrams. Then, when I considered that both diagrams were intended to convey the same sequence of ideas ("the evolution from God to Man"), I was no longer surprised that my own designs should be practically identical with a design which was several thousand years old. I also realized immediately that the Tetragrammaton was just one final layer of abstraction up from the Tree of Life (the Tetragrammaton has always been said to express the same mystery – the evolution from God to Man – although its precise meaning has been universally considered to have been lost over the ages).

So now let us briefly review these ideas. In one way or another, all my writings are expositions of these Arcana, but I will try to review them sufficiently here to lay a basis for understanding the evolution of my ideas of theology. The Number One is the most important, but the hardest to speak about. In the words of the *Tao Te Ching* by Lao Tzu, "From Tao there comes One; from One there come Two; from Two there comes Three; and from Three there come all things." According to Pythagoras, the best illumination of each mystery is contained in the concept of the Number for which it stands. That is, the meaning of the first and most primary mystery can best be understood by meditating on the Number One. The best I can come up with in words is an idea of Perfection expressed as a point which has no dimensions, no existence in time, and, in fact, no existence at all until the universe comes into being by the Error or Joke of a Distinction between All and Nothing, Infinity and Zero (pretending that the two terms mean something different, opposite to each other). Now it is possible to perceive that point of perfection (after the creation of the cosmos) at the center of a sphere of error, or cloud of confusion, surrounding that point. Of course, we can understand that point of Perfection as God (the Holy Ghost, in my most recent understanding of correspondence to the Christian Trinity) and all the manifestation surrounding it as "the Devil." One very important theological point is this understanding of the Devil not as an organized and conscious incarnation of evil (as many Christians seem to believe), but as confusion and error, "distance from God." This makes a whole lot more sense theologically; there are not two gods, one good and one evil (that is an old but primitive idea – compare Zoroastrianism), but only one God, defining Perfection at the center, with Dante's receding circles of Hell the further away one goes from God. God is the light at the center, and "the Devil" is expressed as increasing confusion and error, receding out into chaos, darkness, and death.

But it is a lot more complicated than this. So far we have this pattern of God at the center, with energies of confusion moving out into error. There are numerous applications of this image – for example, we might say that everyone lives their life somewhere on this continuum (which is not linear, but better expressed as a point at the center of a sphere moving out in an infinite number of directions away from God at the center to increasing degrees of error and confusion towards the periphery). Furthermore, it is possible to go closer in towards the center, or to move further out away from God. A practice such as meditation is designed to bring one closer to God, while expressions of anger, over-indulgence in drugs or alcohol, or engaging in crime or war will carry one inexorably further away from God.

So far this might seem to be fairly simple and straightforward – going in is good; going out is bad. But it is not that simple! What we see as error and confusion, iniquity and sin, is actually only the excess of that direction of energy, not any movement in that direction at all! Metaphysically, that direction of energy which caused the universe to break apart from non-being and perfection into manifestation and reality is the Quest for Novelty, which is the Spark of Life! It is an absolutely essential component of the cosmos, and value expressions of "good" or "evil" are wholly inappropriate. One of the reasons why I enjoyed the ideas of Hermetic Alchemy was its recognition that the most efficient path towards perfection was not a bee-line to the center (which, if it were even possible, would just result in the annihilation of all manifestation back into the state of perfect non-being), but the alternation of SOLVE ET COAGULA (breaking apart and coming together). All evolutionary growth is a product of this pattern – inhalation-exhalation, expansion-contraction, analysis-synthesis, etc.

So it is only in excess that this "quest for novelty" gets us into trouble. Initially, this quest for novelty leads to creativity and originality, leading to evolutionary growth and all of the wonders of science and life. However, if the forays out into novelty are not resolved and reintegrated back to the center, the outward moving energy just continues out past creativity and complexity into confusion and madness, eventually leading to chaos, darkness and death.

Now to relate these ideas to the numbers of metaphysics, it is the duality of the Number Two, yang and yin, expansion and contraction. If the Number One represents the ultimate Origin, the reaching out into Novelty of the Number Two represents the spark of life which creates and animates the cosmos. So far from considering this movement "evil," we consider this essential breath of life to be one of the Persons of the Trinity which is God.

At the point of perfection, all good things converge – clarity, harmony, love, joy, bliss, good health, prosperity, etc. Increasing distance away from this point leads to confusion, discord, anger, sorrow, conflict, poor health, failure, etc. Yet, as long as the energy is continually re-integrated back to the center, the movement outward is life itself – novelty, creativity, complexity, and growth. This may seem like a paradox. If all good things converge at the point in the center, how is it that movement away from this point can produce good effects? As I search for an analogy to explain this idea, I find one that may seem unsuitable, yet is really correct. This movement outward, away from the center of perfection is like a drug – coffee, for example. Coffee provides a positive stimulus, yet, in the first place, it is most effective the more rarely it is used. And, secondly, the more it is used to excess, the more negative the effects become. The lesson, then, is that this outward movement is very powerful magic, but it must be used sparingly, and followed by a return back to the center to maintain integrity and balance, to assimilate the new information into the path of evolutionary change and growth. Another very coarse example is spontaneous mutation. Spontaneous mutation is precisely this "quest for novelty" in action, and is the mechanism of evolutionary growth. Yet if the pace of mutation exceeds a safe limit, the organism breaks down into uncontrolled chaos and eventual death. The COAGULA phase must follow the SOLVE in order for the novelties to be either integrated into the center (as the agency of positive growth), or rejected and passed over.

Most Christian theologians consider Jesus as the "Son of God" and the second Person of the Trinity, and none of that is inconsistent with my view. The prime attribute of the convergence of all good things is Love, the ultimate COAGULA. (We must distinguish here, by analogy with mathematics, the "approach to the limit" from "the limit itself." At the actual attainment of the limit, all bets are off, and all manifestation would be hypothetically superseded by non-being.) Since Jesus Christ is unparalleled in the primacy of his message of love, we may say that Jesus was "closer to God" than any other person known to history. I have to take issue here with people who seem to think that the message of Jesus is, "Believe in Me and you will never die." For those who don't know, the message of Jesus can be found in John 13; 34-35 – "A new commandment I give unto you, that ye love one another; as I have loved you, that ye also love one another. By this shall all men know that ye are my disciples, if you have love one to another." And also First John 4:7-8 – "Beloved, let us love one another: for love is of God; and every one that loveth is born of God, and knoweth God. He that loveth not knoweth not God; for God is love."

I find Jesus to be a far more impressive person when understood as a human being who was very close to God, rather than some sort of magical being identified as God Himself. The whole point of the teaching of Jesus was to show the way by example as someone whom we may aspire to follow. Once you claim that he is God Himself his whole existence and message is belittled and trivialized. His followers may have been dazzled, as the Aztecs were dazzled by Cortez and thought he was God, but the story of Jesus makes a lot more sense to me as an example of the power and glory of God the closer we approach to Him. But as close as Jesus was to God, he also embodied the virtues of novelty in large measure! Time after time his message broke with tradition, bringing us, in every way, a New Testament. An example of his attitude is his reply when questioned about healing on the Sabbath: "The Sabbath was made for Man, not Man for the Sabbath. Jesus, being close to God, is a perfect exemplar of the Second Arcanum and the Second Person of the Trinity, reaching out into novelty from the perfection of God.

The funny thing about the Trinity is that it really does take three perspectives to fully understand God. At the top (Arcanum I), there is *God, the Holy Ghost.* Then there are the two forces of the Second Arcanum – *God, the Mother* (yin), and *God, the Son* (yang). Altogether they comprise the Trinity of God.

So if the Number One expresses God as the ultimate Origin, and the Number Two expresses the Divergence into complexity represented by the movement outward into novelty (balanced by movement back in to the center), what is the significance of the Number Three? The Number Three represents the expanding consequence of the divergence of the Number Two. Three is achieved by a point of perspective between Subject and Object. Where the Number Two expresses abstract directions of energy as complementary ideas, the Number Three brings into being an entire field of energy (for example, the entire manifest cosmos and the infinite consciousness of God) which comes into being between the hypothetical and imaginary limits of All and Nothing, Infinity and Zero. This Trinity completes the expression of God. The Number Four represents the actual and tangible manifestation of the cosmos, completing the evolution from God to Man. (More information concerning any of this may be found in my books already mentioned, which may be found on my web site: www.tree.org.)

But let's take a closer look at this Number Three. The key feature of the Third Arcanum is Life and Consciousness. I have developed this idea at greater length in previous writings, but to make a quick summary – by analogy with an atom, which has a nucleus surrounded by a swarm of electrons relatively far out from the nucleus, I imagine that there is a vast field of energy surrounding every human being. Close to the body there may be an aura, visible to some sensitive people, but there must be a huge field of energy extending out for a considerable distance – at least, say, to the outer limits of the atmosphere around planet Earth. What this means is that all life on the planet, human, animal, and vegetable, is occupying the same space! Advancing quickly to a complex idea, I accept the postulate of a being ("Gaia") which is comprised of the entire field of life energy on the planet, with a shared consciousness. Now, by the idea that consciousness increases in direct proportion to the complexity of an organism, Gaia must have a greater consciousness than any of the "separate" people, plants, or animals of which she is composed.

Suddenly all manner of psychic phenomena become very easy to understand, since all life is essentially linked into a single system of energy. You see where I am going with this – it may be that there is a yet larger Being composed of all life in the cosmos, but from our point of view, we may think of Gaia as the Consciousness of God (The Holy Ghost). Suppose this is not just some abstraction, but is actually real? Is it too much to imagine that this Consciousness is "aware" of our individual thoughts on some level?

And what about the other direction? I have always thought it was stupid and useless to "pray" by submitting a shopping list to God like a child writing a letter to Santa Claus. It makes much more sense to me for us to "pray" by listening receptively for any messages which God (or Gaia) may have for us. Perhaps my writings are inspired by God. How was it possible otherwise that I should re-invent the Tree of Life of the Kabbalah so many millennia after its initial appearance? I tuned it in.

Initially I promised an explanation of the creation of the cosmos *ex nihilo*. That requires some extremely dense metaphysical speculation and is actually beyond the scope of the present essay (but see *Speculations on Cosmology*). However, I also promised to resolve the Problem of Evil, which I now propose to do. The resolution of the problem, as Wittgenstein would advise us, is to be found in the statement of the problem itself. "How can we believe in the existence of an Almighty God, infinite in power, wisdom, and goodness, in the face of so much manifest evil in the world?" Well, the solution to the problem lies in the prior assumptions. Who says God is Almighty, infinite in power, wisdom, or even goodness? Are we like the Aztecs dazzled by Cortez, or like children who believe in the infallibility of their parents? If we understand that God is all of Us, all Life on the planet, and We are just trying to stay alive (and, perhaps, losing the battle), then perhaps We can understand the inadequacy of the attitude to "let George do it." We need to take responsibility for Our world, the only one We have, and put Our shoulders to the wheel before it is too late.

Our concept of God has evolved considerably from the Old Testament to the New Testament. Jesus has given us a glimpse of a much greater God than anything found in the Old Testament, by teaching that God is Love; a radical idea then as now. Now it is time for us to come of age and participate in the continuing evolution of God and Man. If we just sit back and let George do it, there may be nothing left for our children. Our planet is dying (and that means We are dying), and it is up to Us to rise to the challenge of Our present need and try to reverse that slide into confusion, error, chaos, darkness, and death. Gaia can't do it without Us. Do you hear Her speaking to you? **If not, then shut up and listen!** At the very least, get out of the way if you can't lend a hand, for the times they are a-changing. It is up to Us to ensure that the changes bring Us closer to the light instead of delivering Us to the rapidly encroaching darkness.

The most urgent priority is to mobilize a vast army of tree planters to restore the protective tree cover on the earth. More trees will improve the carbon balance, produce more oxygen, and help to prevent the destructive cycle of drought and floods by anchoring the soil to the earth, retaining the water when it rains, and returning it gradually during the dry seasons, preventing water runoff and soil erosion. Trees also encourage the survival of smaller shrubs and ground covers, further protecting the earth and its living creatures, including human life.

There are plenty of other problems that need to be addressed, but the restoration of the Trees is such an urgent priority that I don't want to mention anything else on the same page.

The Glory of God is very much manifest in the Trees, but up until now, the human race has just been dragging Us down. The human race has interjected an amazing and explosive burst of Novelty, but if We are unable fully to realize that energy and reintegrate it back to God, it will carry Us inexorably further out along the path of increasing complexity leading to confusion and error, and thence to the outer reaches of chaos, darkness, and death. The message here is that it is not enough to say that "God is in His Heaven, and all's right with the world," or "God works in mysterious ways, but His plan is surely unfolding as it should." No! Our world is spiraling out into chaos, and time is running out. Enough SOLVE already! Now it is time for a new COAGULA to bring Us back to God.

Speculations on Cosmic Consciousness and the Love of God

2016

A while ago (March of 2015) I saw on the news the videos of the soldiers of ISIS destroying all the ancient art, artifacts, and architecture from a museum in Northern Iraq. As I write this, I seem to recall that that was even before the unbelievably egregious destruction of Palmyra a bit later on. All of that is way beyond inexcusable. War is a bad enough business, and, most of the time, both sides seem to be convinced that they are in the right, but wanton destruction of our heritage of ancient art is totally senseless. I am still in shock over the burning of the library at Alexandria, and now this!

Religious beliefs are hard to argue with when people believe on faith the religion they were taught at their mother's knee. When someone else comes along with different beliefs which he also accepts on faith, there is no common ground for any discussion. Well, here I am trying to establish some common ground. My first proposition, which I offer for acceptance as an axiom (accepted without proof) is that "the meaning and purpose of religion is to get closer to God." I believe that is a pretty fundamental idea which most people would accept regardless of their religious backgrounds. Buddhism is not specifically theistic, but I think most Buddhists would accept the proposition anyway, when they see how I understand the concept. (In other words, what I mean by "getting closer to God" turns out to be identical with the goals of Buddhist practice, the attainment of enlightenment being simply equated with union with God.) I can hardly imagine anyone claiming a different purpose for their religious practices, but if they do (e.g., to propitiate an angry God) then my present remarks just do not apply to them.

But, if one accepts my starting premise, then I introduce my second premise, which is that the best way to measure a person's closeness to God is to consider the degree to which they love everyone. I suggest that the most clearly distinguishing feature of the most religious or spiritual people is the love they feel for all of life. Most recognized "holy men" or "holy women" or spiritual teachers are famous for radiating an oceanic love for all life. Once again, it is hard to engage "proofs" for this idea, so I will call it another axiom – "The more love one feels for all of life, the closer one is to God."

So, if we can accept these two propositions, suddenly we have an objective measure of comparison for religious beliefs and practices. Simply look at your religious beliefs and practices and ask, "Do these beliefs and practices bring me closer to God, or do they drive me further away from God? As I continue on the way of my religious observance, am I becoming more loving to all of life, or less?" If one be looking for a spiritual teacher or guru, simply seek one who most clearly radiates the love of God. In other articles, I have repeatedly described a three dimensional continuum which goes from a center of peace, love, harmony, joy, and clarity outwards in all directions towards increasing tension, anger, disharmony, sorrow, and confusion. God is at that point at the center, and the further away one goes from that point, the more one is distant from God ("distance from God" is an old and very good definition for the Devil).

So, to make my conclusion, I say to those soldiers of ISIS,

No, you are not obeying the will of Allah, as you pound those ancient artifacts to rubble, consumed with your passion of anger and hatred. No, you are lost in confusion and error. I am not an Islamic scholar, but I am sure that a diligent search of your Koran will suggest new directions for your energies that might bring you closer to God than your present course of anger, violence, and hatred. It is not necessary to convert to Christianity or Buddhism; all you have to do is seek for those interpretations of your Koran that lead you closer to the love of God.

Of course, it is not only Moslems who drift away from God, seduced by false prophets – plenty of Christians (and others) have lost all understanding of the original teachings of the founders of their Church and are just as lost in confusion and error as any Moslem. I call upon the leaders of every religion to clarify for their communicants the path which leads to the love of God.

Many people are uncomfortable with any expression of religious belief. When I was a child, unbelievers would prudently conceal their unbelief. Now, it is religious believers who hide their beliefs out of a fear of ridicule. Well, the important aspects of my own ideas are quite independent of the religious component. My principle image describing the spiritual state of human beings (a sphere with a center of peace, harmony, clarity, love, and joy extending outward towards increasing anger, disharmony, confusion, hatred, sorrow, darkness, and death) may be applied without any mention of

God. If I label the center "God" and the outer reaches of confusion "the Devil," that may be understood figuratively rather than literally. Certainly the labeling of confusion, distant from God, as "the Devil" is intended to disavow, once and for all, the idea of the Devil as a kind of conscious and deliberate "evil god." And, whether you think of God at the center as a conscious being of some sort or just a figurative image to describe the quality makes no real difference. Just as Buddhist meditation can bring you to a state of peace and serenity, so the effort to become "closer to God" can yield the same benefits of peace, clarity, joy, love, and good health, regardless of any theological ideas pertaining to that mysterious point at the center.

The crux of the whole matter is consciousness. I suggest that consciousness (and free will) increases as you get closer to God (or "to the center") and decreases as you move away into confusion, error, and darkness. So "union with God" would mean the attainment of cosmic consciousness, as well as enlightenment, Nirvana, limitless love, and total bliss. This, of course, is entirely speculative. I am suggesting, by analogy with the consciousness of animals and human beings, that the more complex and highly evolved the organism, the greater the consciousness. To postulate that the entire field of life energy on the planet is all inter-connected and, in fact, comprises a single living being, is also speculative, but it is an extremely interesting and provocative concept, and offers no theological problems whatsoever. It is the suggestion that this being ("Gaia") is fully conscious and is responsible for the nearly universal belief in some sort of God, that is the most radical idea here. If it were true, it could account for a great many unexplained and/or psychic phenomena as a medium for the transmission of all kinds of energies of communication and even telekinetic activity, as well as prayer.

At the same time, it is an idea of God that avoids the deal-breaker concept of an Almighty God Who is responsible for everything that happens in the world, good and bad. When theologians try to explain the Problem of Evil by attempting to shift the blame onto humans, when the Deity should have known better, I don't find their arguments very convincing. I think God is evolving along with Our cosmos, and We are doing the best We can.

Consciousness is a very astonishing experience. But if human beings can enjoy the kind of consciousness with which we are familiar, I do not find it too surprising to imagine Gaia as a conscious being, trying hard to stay alive but losing the battle due to the endless and growing confusion of her parts.

But, whether you believe that Gaia is a conscious Being, an unconscious being, or even just a random and unconnected confusion of unrelated beings (human, animal, and vegetable), the path towards an evolutionary growth that can sustain the fragile envelope of life on this planet is all the same – a concerted effort for all sentient beings to move closer to that center of peace, clarity, love, and joy, regardless of whether you endow that point with any theological significance or not.

Philosophical Meditations

on the Nature of God

2015 - 2017

11.III.15 Suddenly I am re-thinking the whole Gaia hypothesis. The problem is that all of the life energies of the planet do not show a level of integration comparable to the single organism of a person, animal, or plant. It is true that a human being contains millions of smaller organisms that are hostile to the person, and sometimes these hostile organisms destroy the integrity of the person, leading to death. But in this case, those hostile organisms are opposed to the person, not an integral part. I would speculate that the person's consciousness would not include these organisms but would maintain distinction from it. In the same way, a human body sometimes rejects a transplant; the ego (i.e., the center of consciousness) refuses to incorporate the alien part. So, in the case of planet earth, I cannot see the analogy of a single organism with a single consciousness. As I try to make sense of it all, I try to follow the consciousness. I have always had a pagan "many gods" attitude (whether or not there is One overall God) – that every family, school, city, state, tribe, language group, biker group, street gang, or interest group (not to mention every river and forest) may have a shared consciousness, so perhaps our world is just a jungle of such "gods," all struggling for dominance. Perhaps the God of the Hebrews was just that – a parochial god for one tribe of people, not a God who would include other alien tribes (this may be the root cause of much anti-Semitism).

So, if this more accurately represents the spiritual state of the planet, what are the implications for consciousness and/or theology? Of course, I am treading upon unknowable ground, but I am a philosopher, not a scientist. A scientist does not speculate beyond the data, whereas the speculations of philosophers begin where those of the scientists leave off.

My first thought is that I cannot decisively rule out a single consciousness that encompasses all of life. But in view of the jungle of mutually hostile life forms, such a consciousness would not necessarily favor mankind. Perhaps such a consciousness would favor Man's destruction by fire (nuclear war) comparable to an earlier destruction by flood. Once the failed experiment of human life were cleared from the earth, the evolution of life might proceed again, over here, with a fresh opportunity. As to theology, this view of the nature of the consciousness of God does not offer much comfort (to human beings).

But, whether or not there is some sort of overall consciousness, I consider the status of the next level of consciousness down – is there a single consciousness for the human race as a whole, or is the jungle of warring peoples, races, tribes, religions, and lawgivers in an endless struggle for survival or dominance? And what are the implications for the survival of life on earth? Well, as to that, I return to a very old idea of mine, which has been shared by many others over the years – there can be no hope for any positive evolution of the human race until or unless the entire planet be unified under a single political entity. This might be accomplished after devastation by war and conquest, or by political evolution of negotiation and compromise. One idea which I have had from the beginning of my theological speculations about Gaia is that God is just as much a work in progress as any of the life forms which contribute to His consciousness. If the human race and the planet can be unified under a single political structure, then our God could grow commensurately.

So, after all of this speculation, I am left with a world in chaos, beset by warring factions all over the globe with no end in sight. One idea seems clear enough – a gradual and evolutionary movement toward union (COAGULA) is better (i.e., more conducive to the possibility of the survival of life on earth) than a cataclysmic or expanding conflict leading to destruction and chaos (SOLVE).

So, the conclusion of my morning's meditation is to suggest passing out free LSD to all the warring factions all over the world to promote an elevation of spiritual consciousness leading finally to an ultimate union and the triumph of the love of God over the confusion, chaos, and darkness of the Devil.

The lesson for Gaia, the consciousness of our planetary god, is the same as that for every person on the planet – in order to accomplish a positive elevation of spiritual growth, the life energies on our planet, just as with each individual soul, must come together towards a center of clarity, peace, harmony, joy, and love. The alternative, for each person as for our planet, is confusion, destruction, chaos, darkness, and death. "Therefore, choose life." (Deuteronomy 30:15-20)

13.II.15 *Primum Mobile*

I may, of course, be wrong in any of my speculations, but at least I have clear ideas about almost every aspect of philosophy and metaphysics. There is really only one point that is not entirely clear – the very first point, the *primum mobile*. As I have mentioned before, science really has no better explanation for this point than theology. Science can describe the expansion of the Big Bang from the first few millionths of a second after the Big Bang itself, but by that time all of the really interesting stuff is already ancient history. I want to know exactly how and why that Big Bang actually happened in the *first place!* So, that is my problem of metaphysics, and there is also my problem of theology and consciousness – is there a whole planetary consciousness or is the consciousness limited to lower levels? This is unknowable, but my current thinking is that there is some sort of planetary-wide Gaia consciousness, even if the parts are in conflict.

It may sound funny to put it in this way, but, as a God, Gaia is way down on the scale of spiritual evolution (about on the level of the Old Testament God). When the life energies of the planet resemble the fully realized saint of "Buddha Nature" or "Christ Consciousness," then we will be entering a Golden Age or the Kingdom of God on Earth. We have a long way to go (*understatement alert*). So, to clarify my ideas about a personal God Who might hear our prayers or facilitate other psychic phenomena, this might refer to levels of super-consciousness below the planetary level, and these spheres of consciousness may be intermingled in any complex way beyond our comprehension.

But it is the first and most abstract metaphysics that I want to consider now: the *primum mobile* itself. So, to review, there is the First Arcanum, as that point of perfection at the center of our virtual sphere (which doesn't exist until the Second Arcanum brings it into being). Then the Second Arcanum causes the Universe to split apart and come into being with a Quest for Novelty which moves away from the perfection of God at the center outward into "error" in any of an infinite number of directions. Does the First Arcanum have any existence or reality "before" the Second Arcanum brings it all into being? The First Arcanum makes sense to me as a senior concept (from which the Second Arcanum breaks away) even in the absence of the Second Arcanum. In the same sense that the concept of Number may have an *a priori* reality apart from any manifestation in the physical world, so, also, in the same way that we imagine infinity as an approach to a limit, I can imagine an ultimate *ain soph*, total nothingness, as the Original antecedent of the birth of God, which I call the First Arcanum. We might call that *ain soph* the Zero Arcanum, analogous to The Fool of the Tarot.

But it is this Second Arcanum which holds the greater part of my interest! There is something natural and original about the First Arcanum, but the Second Arcanum is really the trigger (or its consequence) which initiates the Big Bang. [The First Arcanum and the Second Arcanum are different; The *Change* which happens occurs at a point between the two Arcana, in the same way that the First Arcanum already expresses the point in process as it changes from *ain soph* to the first singularity.]

So what is this Quest for Novelty, and whence does it come? It doesn't seem to be as obvious a given as the serenity and perfection of the First Arcanum. The Quest for Novelty exists because without it there would be nothing to disturb the serenity of God's infinite Perfection. But *why* does it exist? It is, obviously, the origin and source of life, as well as all existence, personified as *Eros*. In spite of the fact that it is clearly a "junior" concept to the seniority and perfection of the First Arcanum, it seems to be responsible for most of the interest. The movement inward, back to the center and perfection of God, seems to be more like a resolution of the error implied by the movement away from the center (this would be gravity – time and/or space is "the measure of error") but the movement outward, in any of an infinite number of directions in search of novelty, seems to bear all of the dynamic potential of the cosmos and of life. (It also offers a theoretical explanation for the significance of "devil worship.")

So this Quest for Novelty is the final and irreducible *primum mobile*, after all. It defies speculation as to where It might come from – all we can say is that without It there never would have been any universe to disturb the Perfection of God.

Nothing in these speculations is contrary to any of the findings of science – all I have done is to restore the name of God to the Creation. Until any scientist or theologian can explain the how or why of the Big Bang at the moment of Creation itself, I will prefer my solution, as it showcases the very focal point of the Mystery Itself instead of trying to pretend that it doesn't exist.

16.XII.16 Another explanation for the *primum mobile* might claim that the quest for novelty is inherent in the metaphysics. By analogy, we claim that the numbers of mathematics may be entirely derived *a priori* and *ex nihilo.* The concept and meaning of the numbers of mathematics do not depend upon any external realities. In the same way, it may be possible to claim that the metaphysics of the sequence of the primary mysteries of nature is also inherent in the fundamental nature of reality. The metaphysical expansion of the ideas of Number have been there all along, as much a part of the attributes of Number as their use as simple counting markers. Specifically, as the Second Arcanum reaches Outward into Novelty it is nothing more nor less than the inevitable expression of the Second Arcanum. In the same way, the Mystery of the Number Three is just as inevitable: once the process of expansion into complexity through the operation of the Quest for Novelty has begun (SOLVE ET COAGULA), it will inevitably generate Life, and, finally, Consciousness. You can call this God, or just call it the natural world doing its thing.

A very interesting idea from Taoism is *enantiodromia:* reversal *in extremis,* the idea that as everything makes its round of cyclical progression, at the end of every extremity of yang or yin there is a turning around to go the other way. This is the same as the Quest for Novelty and the Return to the Center, or the *Solve et Coagula* of the alchemists. According to this view, the universe had to pop into existence sooner or later, and, as time is meaningless in the absence of existence, it just had to happen. Now, of course, the universe is winding back down to Nothingness once again. This cycle of a universe popping into and out of existence may be analogous to the popping into and out of existence of sub-atomic particles of quantum physics.

On the other hand, it is possible to imagine that this is all Natural and inevitable, and doesn't require any "God" to put it into motion. Or, you could say that the bursting apart of Original Perfection into the endless Quest for Novelty and the Return to the Center, is God's little Joke, and it is His Laughter that we know as the unfolding Universe. This would be God's way of existing forever without getting bored.

10.I.17 *Deus fecit*

Looking over these meditations, I can see that I have narrowed it down to two possibilities – either we accept the premise that the metaphysical extensions of the concept of Number are, in fact, as inherent in the numbers themselves as are their qualities as simple counting units, so that the whole progression of metaphysics is inevitable – that the universe just had to pop into existence "sooner or later," and that the evolution to life and consciousness was also inevitable; or one could deny the associations of metaphysics to the qualities of Number. In fact, one might even reject the claim that Number itself could be derived *a priori* and *ex nihilo*. My metaphysics falters on the same rock that stumps the scientist. Certainly, given One, Two must follow, and then Three, and then All Things. But who says the One is given? If even the abstractions of Number be not allowed as given (or as axioms), then the Original Source of the initial One is just as unknown as the hypothetical Big Bang of science.

But that is all good – if the claim that the metaphysics is inherent in the concept of Number be not considered sufficient to say that the universe made itself, then Whatever or Whoever brought it into being, we might as well call God.

The concept of *enantiodromia* is the foundation of Taoism. It is even a definition of the Tao, as in "From Tao there comes One . . ." [I], which started off the whole chain of events. The dichotomy and alternation of All and Nothing, Infinity and Zero [II], is inevitable, and the alternation between the two sets up a field of energy between them [III] which, in turn, creates the manifest cosmos [IV]. Zero and Infinity may be equivalent at the limit, but in the hypothetical movement between the two a whole potential field of energy comes into being, reaching out into Novelty, hence the ensuing evolution into the cosmos as we know it.

So we can trace the origin of the cosmos back to the Tao. But, of course, whence comes this Tao? I think it is irreducible. Either we accept the Tao as original and fundamental, out of which the cosmos created itself, or we append the name of a causal agent: *Deus fecit*. It's all one.

29.I.17

The fundamental axiom of Western Logic is that "A Proposition is either True or False." From this axiom, the whole system of mathematics, philosophy, and science is deduced analytically. In the binary logic of computers, each bit in the string is either On or Off. This may seem straightforward enough, and, like Newtonian physics, it generally suffices for most of the tasks to which Western logic is put.

But, just as Western logic and mathematics prove inadequate when dealing with sub-atomic or quantum levels of reality, they are also inadequate when dealing with macrocosmic questions such as the creation or origin of the universe. No, for those questions we must employ the more comprehensive potential of Eastern logic and philosophy.

Where the Western philosopher or scientist takes as his starting axiom that a proposition is either true or false, the Eastern philosopher allows for a proposition to be either "True," "Not True," "both True and Not True," or "neither True nor Not True."

Careful analysis of the last two possibilities reveals that they are essentially the same, but from the point of view of opposite perspectives. Thus, we can simplify the Eastern position by suggesting that there is a "Third Way" in addition to the two values recognized by Western logic, philosophy, and science.

This "third way" throws an enormous monkey wrench into any effort to get a grasp on reality. To begin with, we must regretfully give up the concept of "certainty." We can never be certain of anything, at all. To get an idea of what it might mean in terms of our efforts to understand the cosmos, I want to combine the ideas of Heraclitus and Lao Tzu. From Heraclitus we get the idea that nothing can exist without the simultaneous existence of its opposite. From Lao Tzu and the concepts of Taoism we get the idea that Yang and Yin succeed each other in turn. So we might evolve a new idea, that, to start with the binary logic of computers, each bit is either "predominantly On," "predominantly Off," or "fluctuating so rapidly between On and Off that its state is indeterminate."

In the ordinary reality of daily life, these fluctuations mostly balance each other out, but on the level of quantum mechanics or macro-cosmology, the indeterminate nature of reality is inescapable. This is the loophole that "lets the magic in," allowing our cosmos to exist at all, with the possibility of expanding towards limitless complexity in search of endless novelty.

So, sit back and watch the show, or sit up and participate in the unfolding of our astonishing universe.

29.IX.17

Question – is Enantiodromia (reversal *in extremis*, the Tao) sufficient to explain the Quest for Novelty? Or is the Quest for Novelty the elder idea, which requires the utilization of the principle of Enantiodromia, the Tao, to implement its intention?

It seems to me that I have failed to find a First Cause sufficient to create the universe *ex nihilo*. My candidate, the Tao, is silent when asked whence he comes. So if we say that the Quest for Novelty utilizes the Tao to obtain its effects, the position of this Quest for Novelty is sounding more and more theological all the time. But I can't think of any other way to account for it. Otherwise, if we say that the Quest for Novelty is derived from the Tao, it is the same situation, just calling the First Cause by a different name. *Deus fecit*.

24.X.17

My problem has always been the *Primum Mobile* – how did it all begin?

I have a metaphysics which explains the endless expansion into complexity that is our universe, but I feel like the scientist who describes the original expansion of the cosmos from the Big Bang, beginning ten millionths of a second after the big bang happened – who cares about those minor details? I want to know *how it all began.*

The sequence of the *Arcana* are as fundamental and *a priori* as the numbers of mathematics.   The Primary Mysteries, illuminating the unfolding evolution from God to Man, are inherent in the Numbers, as Pythagoras so famously figured out so long ago. And the sequence of the first four comprise the Tree of Life of the Kabbalah, and the Name of God, the *Tetragrammaton.* Why, it is enough to make one give up eating beans (as required by followers of the school of Pythagoras).

So far, all of this is the answer to the question, "Where do all of these ideas come from?" So we are only really left with one problem – why did the Big Bang happen to have happened when it did? Actually, this is the easier question – obviously "time" has no more meaning than anything else prior to the moment of creation.

As to these unfolding Mysteries, starting from Arcanum 0, the *ain soph,* then all three of the primary *Arcana* come into being at once – I, II, and III. Then comes IV, the manifestation of our cosmos springing to life *ex nihilo,* as the consequence of the metaphysics set up by the first three, followed by the endless expansion into complexity, which is still going on. ("This trip is going on.")

The sequence of the *Primary Arcana* are a description and illumination of the unfolding evolution from God to Man, just as the sequence of primary numbers expresses the same thing more abstractly. The *Tetractys* of Pythagoras, the *Tree of Life* of the *Kabbalah*, and the four letters of the Hebrew Name of God (*Tetragrammaton*), are all expressions of the first four primary mysteries.

22.XII.17

Contemporary binary logic suggests a linear sequence of points, each of which is On or Off, just as Western Logic assumes that a Proposition is either True or False.

Suppose, as an alternative logic, a non-linear succession of points, each of which is either On, Off, or Indeterminate (True, False, or neither/both). Thence proceeds a triangular logic of great complexity, leading to a whole new world of logical possibility.

[2018: This may not be just a crazy and impossible idea of mine; I have recently (long after first writing those words above) been reading about "Quantum Computers" featuring "qubits" which "are capable of being in both states at the same time – 1 or 0").]

27.XII.17

What non-binary logic might look like as applied to our own world –

Binary: On, Off, On, Off, On, Off . . .

Non-Binary: at random intervals, a point might be *Indeterminate*, which would then be followed by either On or Off, or both.

. . . On, Off, *Ind.* --> On, Off, On, Off . . . --> Off, On, Off, On . . .

This is the flaw in Perfection that "lets the magic in," and perhaps allows our Cosmos to come into being at all. If, at any point, a link in an energy stream becomes indeterminate, it can be followed by going in either direction, on or off, true or false. The possibility of this happening can be entirely random, or there may be an average "cosmological constant novelty factor." It seems to me that the indeterminacy must be totally random; otherwise, it makes no sense at all.

The first bifurcation of Reality, from infinite Perfection to the endless interplay of Yang and Yin, All or Nothing, was the spontaneous Creation of the Cosmos. Since then, this potential for novelty has kept our world expanding outward into endless unfolding complexity and further growth.

A One World Total Make-Over

being a re-statement of my plan to save the world

2016

Well, at least I'm not the only one. I wonder why this world is in such a terrible mess when so many people are crying out about all the problems. But crying out is not enough; pointing out all the problems does not advance the argument very much at all. In order for any *change* to happen, someone has to *do* something.

I have always found myself thinking about the largest and most serious problems of the world. Whenever any problem appears, I always want to go to the root of the problem – the ultimate root – because it has always seemed to me to be so much energy wasted if you do not address the most important and fundamental issues first.

It is perfectly clear that the single most important issue, from the point of view of the survival of life on earth, is the ongoing collapse of our very fragile eco-system in the biosphere of our little wandering planet. (*Plant more trees!*)

But before any of those issues can be adequately addressed on a planet-wide basis, it is necessary to forge a political union of the whole earth. Yes, of course – *One World Government,* and *A New World Order.* It is not surprising that everyone is so terrified of this, because the obstacles to such a cataclysmic and potentially explosive change in the fundamental stability of the earth are so enormous that no one can think of any way to proceed. But the problems of the world are not going to be solved with baling wire, Scotch tape, black thread, or mirrors, let alone chewing gum, and any efforts in those directions are totally useless while our planet is dying all around us. What this planet needs is a total make-over from the top. Unless we shoulder the responsibility ourselves, the only hope for the earth is *deus ex machina* – literally. Otherwise, there is no future for this little world at all. Our world is rapidly falling apart on all sides, driven by the biological processes of our dying planet, and exacerbated by the ensuing and compounding ecological, social, political, and economic collapse all around us.

In fact, the only possible solution to this problem must be theological. It was not for nothing that the old kings used to claim to rule by divine right, since it is clear that the only source of authority must come from God. But that, of course, is the crux of the whole problem – who will convey and certify the Word of God to Man?

How could any of the diverse nations in the world agree to give up their sovereignty to any other entity? And yet, a solution to the problem has to be found – and I found one over forty years ago that I still think is the best and only possible solution (if you have a better idea, put it forward; don't wait). And that is to create a Seminary of children selected at a young age from all over the world to form a **School of International Studies** that would be fully endowed to cover all the expenses of the students, the teachers, and all additional staff. It would be dedicated to an on-going in-depth study of the world's problems, region by region. In addition to the best possible regular teachers, there would be an on-going program of different specialists making special presentations to the students. Then, at some future time (perhaps thirty years later), the seminary would meet together and choose one of their number to represent them as the instrument to interpret and execute the Will of God on Earth. He or she would then appoint members of a new seminary to ensure a stable continuity.

This idea of the seminary is like an alchemical vessel, and the intent and purpose is literally to conjure an Incarnation and Avatar of God. If this sounds like an exercise in Classical Magic, you are entirely correct; that is just exactly what it is. But it is not Black Magic – it is not the furtherance of our own will that is sought, but a vehicle through which, once again, God's Voice may be heard on our Planet, in Her time of need.

You might think that all of that is a tall order, and quite enough for one day's work, but that is only the one single most pressing problem of our day; there are others. For example, after the Source of Authority be established and a World Government be instituted under the direction of this new Avatar, who will speak with God's Voice – (this plan was first suggested at the establishment of the **Church of the Living Tree** [*quod vide:* www.tree.org], and this Avatar of God was called "The Advocate for the Tree") – after all of this has been arranged, it is time to address the third most pressing problem (after the Source of Authority, and the Biological Restoration of our planet) – Economics, the basis and nature of Money.

At present, the jungle of Money is just as serious and wild a problem as the political chaos on the ground. This prevailing economic jungle is a holdover from the days of feudalism (money being simply a liquid form of property), with sources of capital concentrating in fewer and fewer hands all the time, while the rest of the world is dying of poverty, starvation, and war.

The solution here for a brand new make-over of the world financial system is comparable to the political solution, and, in fact, becomes its primary arm of implementation for its policies.

First of all, instead of money being understood from the point of view of debt, I think it should be understood as credit. The World Government, under the authority of the **Advocate for the Tree** (or whatever he might be called) would create and issue credit as needed, denominated in a new currency. These days, most financial transactions are done by computer, but there would also be some issuance of paper currency, as needed.

To start with, other currencies would be honored for a determined value in the new currency. Other currencies, however, would be deliberately devalued over time to expedite the economic transfer to the new world currency. The value would be easily maintained and adjusted by means of a universal tax on property, which would be taken annually and which would have to be paid in the new currency. All other taxes would be eliminated, except for those that come under the heading of "Resource Depletion Taxes." Otherwise, there would be an entirely free market, with no business taxes or income taxes, with everyone free to pursue their own road to financial independence and security.

For those who run out of money or resources, a network of Free Farms would be set up for the housing and feeding of the indigent. Schools would be free, and hospitals and health care would be largely subsidized. Inner city transit trains and buses would run for free. Anything which needed to be done anywhere in the world would simply be paid for by the State. I can also imagine that the State would run non-profit food stores, clothing stores, and hardware stores. Anyone would be free, of course, to set up any competing markets, probably by providing specialty items not found in the government stores.

The rate of the universal property tax would be determined by the optimum amount of the money supply. The interesting thing about this economic system is that the government would simply create whatever money it needs. Then, when taxes are collected, they would be automatically removed from the property owners' accounts with the World Bank. Where would the "money" go? It would simply be annihilated, roughly balancing out the funds created by the government constantly as it goes about its business, addressing problems and needs as they occur in the world. Private investment banks would be perfectly legal, but the World Bank would pay no interest and charge no fees – and it would certainly not "bail out" any failing banks!

Some people may think that this is just a form of Communism, and it is true that it incorporates many features of that political and economic philosophy, but where it differs is in the complete freedom of everyone to participate in the free market in any way he or she wishes – most of the really important and innovative products and services would always be provided by the private sector, and there would always be new opportunities unfolding as our world evolves.

Most Americans take it as an article of faith that Democracy, as enshrined in the Constitution, is the best form of government ever devised.

Many people are willing to admit that there are some flaws in the system, but the inevitable conclusion is that "In spite of its flaws, American Democracy is still better than any known alternative."

Well, the U.S. Constitution was a product of its times, and was admirably suited to the needs of the fledgling State. However, as Thomas Jefferson himself so insightfully recognized, the longer any government persists, the more it will be taken over by an Establishment of wealth and power that cares more (– a lot more; try "exclusively cares") about the preservation and enhancement of its own wealth and power than about any other concerns of the country or its "little people."

This has become more and more dramatically evident as the years roll by. Democracy might have been a good idea, but we don't live in a Democracy anymore, except in name. The System that has evolved in the U.S.A. is a "Capitalist Plutocracy." And now, as I write in January of 2017, we have a Capitalist Plutocrat as our President-elect who seems to be intending to make America great again for the 1%, while the rest of us run very fast trying to stay in the same place, and our world slips ever more deeply into necrosis. The trees are gone; the topsoil is gone; the animals and honeybees are dying off; the oceans are dying; the polar ice caps are melting. (I understand you can pick up prime ocean-front property in Bangla Desh for a song and a dance.) The death of our planet and the survival of life on earth just don't seem to rate as very high priorities to the ones holding the ownership of the planet in their portfolios.

So, I venture to suggest that the political chaos in the world is not limited to the Middle East, but is a systemic problem the whole world over, including our own little corner of it. Our Constitution has outlived its usefulness, and our system has become corrupted just as Thomas Jefferson predicted that it would be. It is not only time for a new political institution in this country, but the citizens of the world cannot afford to wait any longer before a whole new Contract be worked out that encompass a vision for the entire planet, and entrust the executive authority of the planet to a carefully considered institution that will safeguard the health of the planet and the rights and welfare of its citizens, for the benefit of future generations.

Yes, there are plenty of problems yet remaining, but nothing much can be done about them until these three big ones are accomplished.

Oh – how are these little improvements going to be introduced to the world, you ask? I never said it was going to be easy, yet there is a way – the keystone of the arch is this hypothetical Seminary. Well, that can be started immediately, as soon as funding becomes available to endow the institution with operating funds. Then the world will have thirty years or so to get used to the idea. During those years, all existing problems will probably be getting a lot worse (declining state of the world's eco-system as the dying planet causes continuing climate change, political chaos, economic chaos, over-population, demographic changes, etc.), so that this new Avatar of God may be recognized and welcomed for what he or she would be – a last chance to heal the planet, evolving into a sane, safe, and stable world, where all of our children might have one more chance to stay alive.

The Noosphere

March, 1917

I am just reading over *The Phenomenon of Man* by Pierre Teilhard de Chardin, one of the most significant books in the history of philosophy. His thesis is that the evolution of the universe is the evolution of Life, and that the evolution of Life leads inevitably to the evolution of Consciousness.

He sees this evolution on an inevitable trajectory towards an increasing of consciousness towards some unknowable future state which he calls the Omega Point. He leaves it there, not hazarding a speculation as to the nature of such a point, but he understands it as a transformational point by which ontogenesis, biogenesis, and noogenesis make a major breakthrough to a whole new plateau, as profound as the initial transformation into Life from the chance agglomerations of matter, or the transformation into the level of reflective thought and consciousness from the instinctive level of lower animals

Today's meditation is a speculation as to the nature of that evolutionary advance which will lead life and consciousness into these new levels of experience.

I suggest that this transformational point which we are in the process of crossing is the transition from individual consciousness to planetary-wide bio-consciousness. Actually, Teilhard de Chardin suggested as much, but he clearly anticipates that there will be much about this new experience that is beyond speculation. This evolutionary leap may take a great many years to be fully accomplished, but I expect that we will see more and more people sharing a planetary-wide consciousness as the years go by. Together we will form a whole new plateau in the expression of Life leading to monumental changes in every aspect of our existence.

I have always felt that I were "tuning in" messages from the planetary-wide "Gaia consciousness," not only in terms of philosophical ideas, but also in terms of planetary evolution. Now, some of my ideas may seem way beyond radical (*vide, e.g., A Total World Makeover*), but eventually the ideas may be accepted as inevitable.

Economic Theory

May, 2017

I am reading the very disturbing book *The Shock Doctrine* by Naomi Klein, which is a scathing indictment of Milton Friedman's Free Market theories. I compare the economic implications with my own economic recommendations as outlined in my writings (*vide, e.g., A One World Total Makeover*, 2016).

The fundamental problem of economics (as in politics, as clearly understood by Thomas Jefferson) is that, *regardless of the economic or political system*, the longer the game goes on, the more the wealth and power become concentrated in fewer and fewer hands. This isn't any new revelation – Jesus Christ put it quite succinctly: "To those who have, more shall be given; from them who have not, it shall be taken away even the little that they have."

As long as this universal truth be clearly understood, there is no difficulty understanding political or economic evolutions, nor is it difficult to see what needs to be done to ameliorate the unfortunate consequences of that truth.

Milton Friedman's religiously fundamentalist belief in the sanctity of free markets is not hard to understand, as long as you are prepared to accept a ruthless and unreconstructed Darwinist approach to civilization and life itself. Free markets, without any pesky regulation or controls, will certainly stimulate surging market economies. This "surging market economy," however, is only enjoyed by 20%, or 10%, or 1% of the total population; the remainder of the population (the "little people") is of no consequence or interest to the market leaders and winners.

Where this theory breaks down, of course, is with the same limits encountered by any other invasive pestilence – its very success is its undoing: when the host is destroyed, the growth feeding on it will also die.

My own economic suggestions seem to me to follow just the right line – allowing an unfettered free market in order to enjoy the efficiencies inherent in the free market, but tempered with extensive support for the other 80%, 90%, or 99% of the population. Thus, I have called for the implementation of Free Farms providing free housing, food, education, and health care for the indigent, along with a complete program of support for everyone else – free inner city trains and buses, subsidized food stores and health care, etc.

Of course, the excesses of the free market would also be directly limited with my proposed Resource Depletion Tax, whose levels would be adjusted as necessary to promote market modifications. For example, facing the potentially catastrophic consequences of Climate Change, we would rapidly ratchet up a carbon tax that would make coal fired power plants totally unprofitable, and gasoline a very expensive fuel for automobiles. Air travel would likewise be so expensive that only the wealthiest persons would use it, and then only for the most essential transportation needs (importing Maine lobster, for example . . .). The tax for cutting down a tree would be so high that forest products would become prohibitively expensive, forcing the development of alternative products. Wind, solar, and geothermal power would very quickly replace 20th Century reliance on fossil fuels.

But with all of this support for the poorer members of society, the wealthy class could be free to develop whatever products and services they could manage to sell to each other or anyone else, on a free market basis, without excessive business taxation or other interference in their activities (beyond the resource depletion tax).

None of this will happen automatically, nor does it make any sense to hire a fox to guard the hen house (*e.g.,* Donald Trump) – every garden needs a Gardener to maintain the healthiest balance of life in the garden or the world, and our suggestion of setting up an independent institution (*e.g.,* **The Seminary** of **The Church of the Living Tree**) to produce a source of regulatory authority still sounds good to me. It seems to me that the holders of wealth and power in the world ought to welcome such an independent authority, recognizing that without it there would be no restraint to prevent the destruction of the host – in this case, our dear Mother Earth.

TETRAGRAMMATON

The Keys of the Arcana

The Theory of Everything

by John Roland Stahl

to future generations
of life on earth

ISBN: 978-0-945303-22-0

THE ARCANA

Hermetic Philosophy is the Process of Change. Pythagorean Philosophy is the Ultimate Nature of Reality, and the Meaning of Life.

Mathematics is the Language of God. Pythagoras suggested that it is an expanding Pattern expressing and revealing the Ultimate Nature of Reality. The sequence of Natural Numbers corresponds to the same sequence of the Principle Mysteries of Life in the order of their Importance; and the Keys to these Mysteries are the Numbers themselves.

The sequence of the first four Numbers and their associated Mysteries is the basis of the Tree of Life of the Hebrew Kabbalah. The Tetragrammaton, the four letters of the Name of God, represents the same sequence of Numbers and Mysteries. Pythagoras called the same sequence of ideas Tetractys, represented as pictured on the Title Page.

Heraclitus had the idea that Nothing could exist as a Thing in Itself, but could only exist by the simultaneous existence of its opposite. We expand this idea by combining it with the Taoist principle that the directions of Yang and Yin (On and Off, expanding towards Infinity and contracting towards Zero), succeed each other in turn, as when reaching the Limit in either direction, they turn to go the other way (enantiodromia: Tao).

The Appearance of the Universe is the fluctuation between All and Nothing, the endless Patterns of which thence ensuing evolving eventually to produce Life and Consciousness, on its way to endless expansion into further Novelty and ever increasing Complexity.

We are alive.

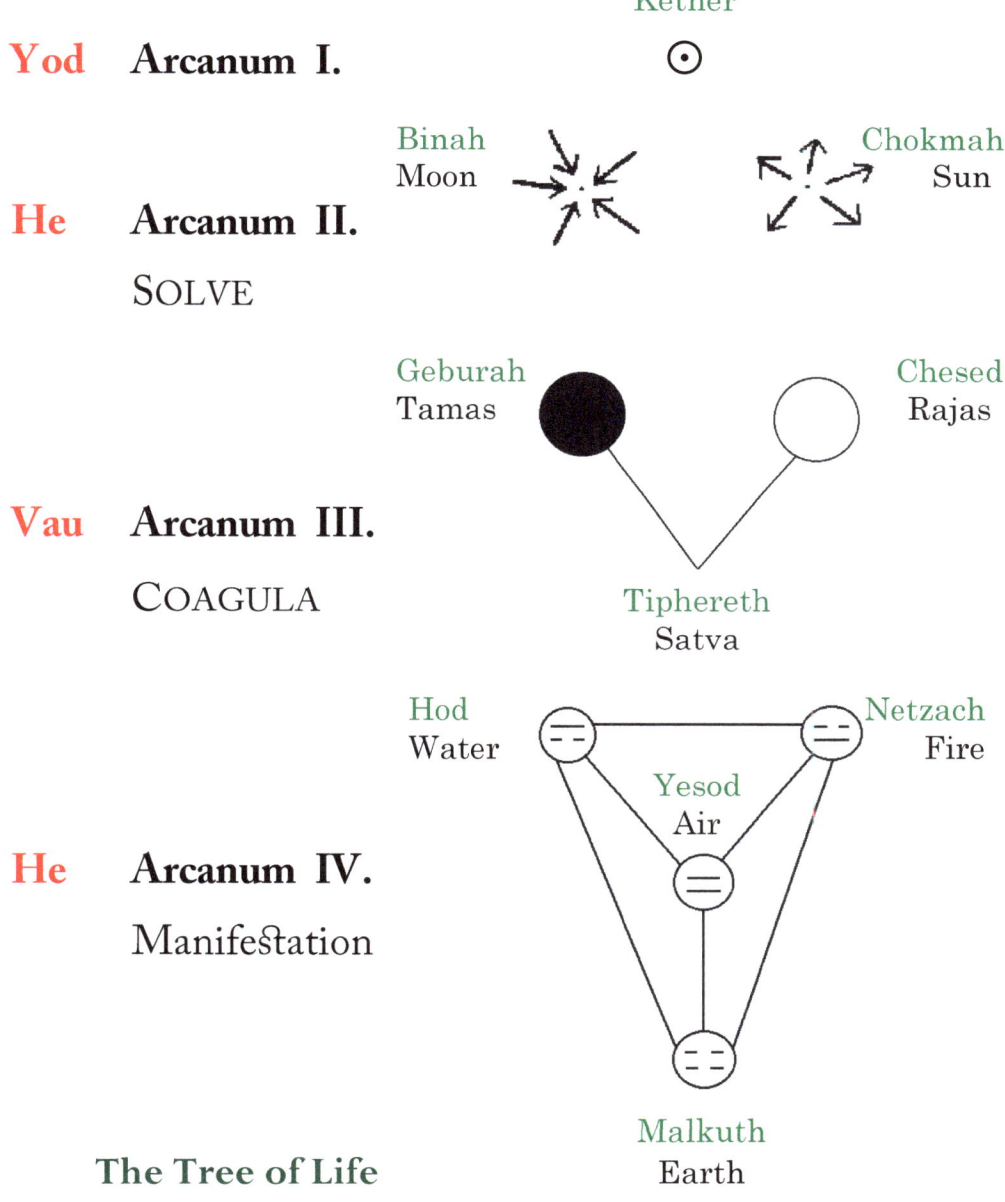

Yod   **Arcanum I.**

Kether

He   **Arcanum II.**

SOLVE

Binah — Moon

Chokmah — Sun

Vau   **Arcanum III.**

COAGULA

Geburah — Tamas

Chesed — Rajas

Tiphereth — Satva

He   **Arcanum IV.**

Manifestation

Hod — Water

Netzach — Fire

Yesod — Air

Malkuth — Earth

The Tree of Life

ARCANUM 0

ain soph

•

ARCANUM I

Yin

— —	——
Yin	Yang
Passive	Active
Contraction	Expansion
Receptive	Creative
Inertia	Novelty
Gravity	Force
Apollo	Dionysus
God	Eros
Positional Chess	Combinational Chess
Theology	Metaphysics
COAGULA	SOLVE

Arcanum II

Yang

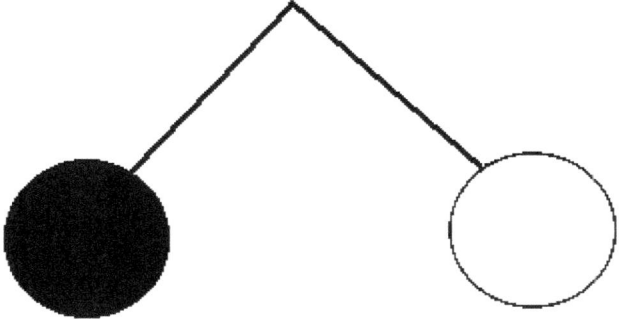

"From Tao there comes One.
From One there come Two.
From Two there comes Three.
From Three there come all things."

~ Lao Tzu
Tao Te Ching

ARCANUM III

Tao

Wands
Yesod
Air
SUMMER
Old Yang
_____
_____

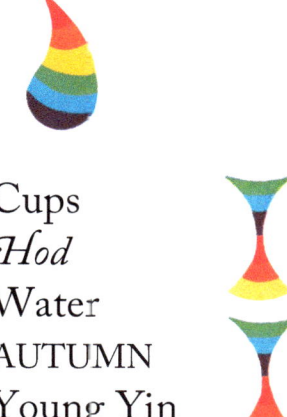

Cups
Hod
Water
AUTUMN
Young Yin
_____
___   ___

Swords
Netzach
Fire
SPRING
Young Yang
___   ___
_____

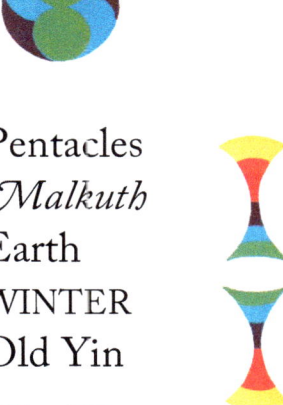

Pentacles
Malkuth
Earth
WINTER
Old Yin
___   ___
___   ___

ARCANUM IV

Life

As Above,

The Present Moment   *Lapis Philosophorum*

So Below.

ARCANUM V

Change

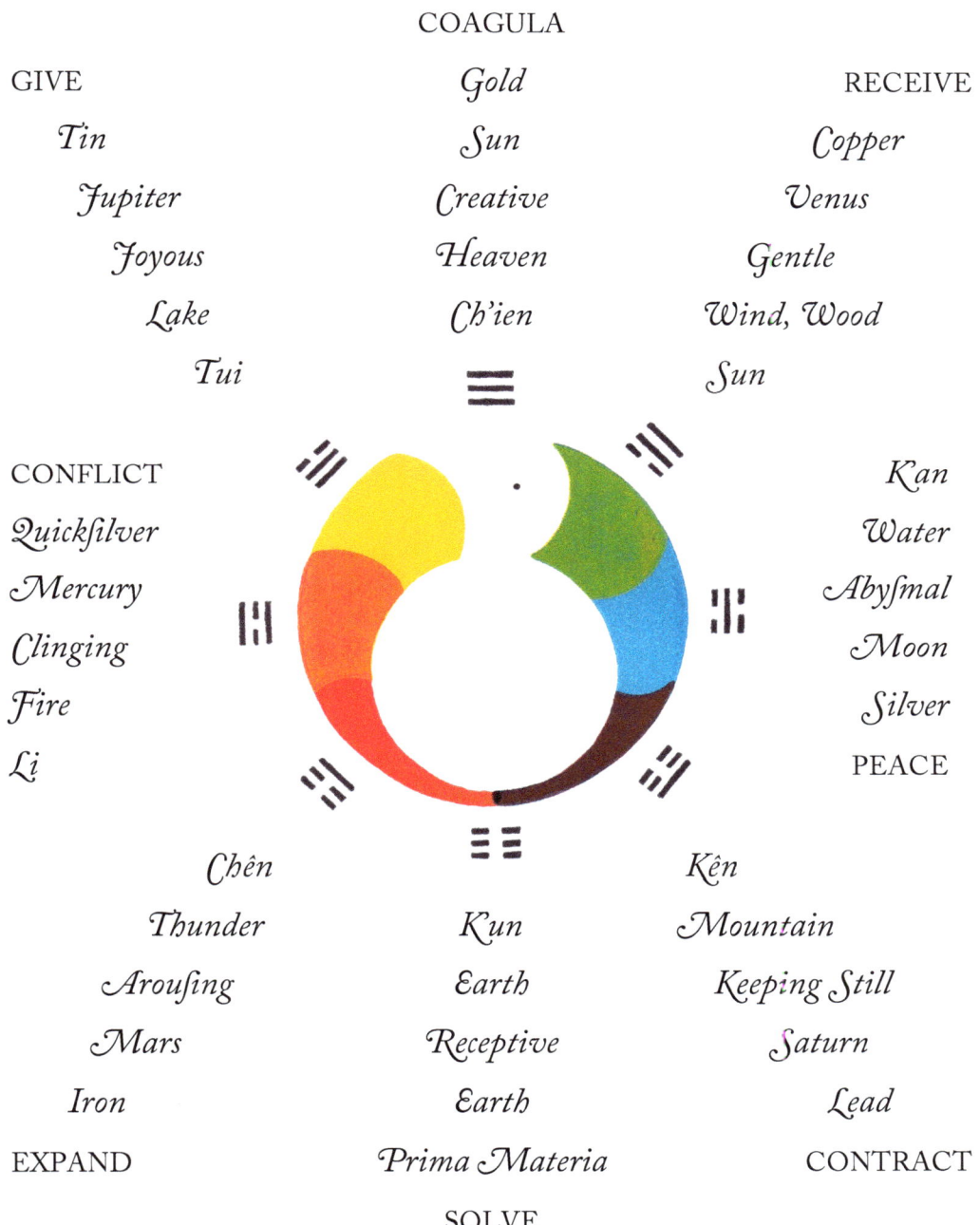

COAGULA

GIVE   Gold   RECEIVE

Tin   *Sun*   *Copper*

Jupiter   *Creative*   *Venus*

Joyous   *Heaven*   *Gentle*

Lake   *Ch'ien*   *Wind, Wood*

Tui   *Sun*

CONFLICT   *Kan*

Quicksilver   *Water*

Mercury   *Abysmal*

Clinging   *Moon*

Fire   *Silver*

Li   PEACE

Chên   *Kên*

Thunder   *Kun*   *Mountain*

Arousing   *Earth*   *Keeping Still*

Mars   *Receptive*   *Saturn*

Iron   *Earth*   *Lead*

EXPAND   *Prima Materia*   CONTRACT

SOLVE

God – Life – Light
Consciousness – Free Will – Health
Love – Harmony – Peace
Clarity

*Expansion
into Novelty*

Creative
Yang

*Contraction
to the Center*

Receptive
Yin

Confusion
Hatred – Anger - Conflict
Chaos – Karma – Disease
The Devil – Death – Darkness

Guns or Money?

July, 2016

The Chinese figured out long ago that it isn't about guns anymore; it's about money. The Americans don't seem to have figured that out yet. Even bin Laden famously understood perfectly well what he was doing – the intent was to bankrupt Uncle Sam, and it's been working beautifully. The Americans gleefully ratchet up their debt into astronomical trillions waging war all over the world, while the Chinese bankers have been quietly picking up the paper. Nothing is made in the United States anymore except weapons, meaning that its industries flourish in times of international tension and war; everything else is made in China.

Change happens very gradually at two points, and changes very suddenly at the other two points. The first Change is a sudden one as something New bursts into being. The second Change, however, happens very gradually – as the original, expansive energy begins to wane, the reversal turning back down happens very slowly. The third Change is another sudden one, in which death supervenes. The fourth Change, completing the cycle, is very gradual, as the *prima materia* begins to draw together the energy to form a new life again.

So, if we apply this description of the process of life and death to the economic and political life of the planet, at what stage is the United States, or the Earth as a whole, on that cycle of life and death? Well, the United States is clearly in decline. There can be no doubt about it – neither its political nor its economic systems are up to the challenges of the present day. As to the question of the political process, Donald Trump is the *reductio ad absurdum* to that one. But its economic system is equally inadequate. Free market capitalism is out of control, and must be restrained. There must be an independent government establishment that is not beholden to any special interests at all. This would be my idea of a seminary of students selected from all over the country (or the world) to hold the Sovereign Authority in trust. If they are given the best possible education, they will surely select the best one of their number to exercise the sovereign authority. My idea of making the sovereign authority identical with the Bank is practically a matter of definition, as the power to create money at will is a virtually unlimited power.

I see three stages in the implementation of this plan. First, there is the establishment of the Seminary. This can be done without any political importance at all – it is simply a matter of funding. As soon as adequate funding be available, a seminary can be constituted and launched, and its students can begin to receive the best possible education, completely liberated from any of the ordinary pressures of life. Specialists in all fields will make specially prepared presentations to the class, so they will benefit from the best available sources of information. Their curriculum will be overseen by a team of scholars in all fields who will make sure that all of the most important information be included in their studies.

The next stage of the process would begin when someplace on the earth, some sovereign state, decides to vest a new currency in the institution of the Seminary and the person of the Advocate. For example, Greece may continue its endless and long drawn out bankruptcy, continuing to pile up impossible loans and obligations to the IMF, the European Central Bank, and others; or it might simply declare bankruptcy, repudiate all debt, and institute a new currency, created at will on demand by the Seminary's Advocate, agreeing as well to pay all property taxes back to the State as represented by the Bank of the new currency.

If the enterprise be a failure, of course there will be nothing more heard of this funny idea, but if it survives and flourishes, other countries may want to opt in, at which point the citizens and companies will exchange their current money into the new currency, again agreeing to pay their property taxes to the new bank.

This third stage of evolution and growth can continue for as long as necessary, leading to one or another of several possible end games – the new State might swell to world status relatively unchecked, or there might be one or several significant hold-outs opposing the world union. Well, in that case, it would simply become an economic contest between the sovereign nations. How can you have an economic contest against a country that prints up money at will? But that is no problem – obviously, the more money there is, the less it is worth, so the economic contest would remain real. Then, either the hold-out countries gradually enter the union, or they manage to stay viable independently. If that is the case, there is no reason why independent states couldn't continue to exist indefinitely. In fact, it is almost inevitable that an opposition will always be present, and this is probably a good thing. Or, at least, it will be a manifestation of the Tao, so we might as well accept it.

A Run on Uncle Sam?

August, 2017

I am reading a lot of Noam Chomsky these days, after reading a lot of Bertrand Russell, and there is no way to escape the fact that the United States has become more and more of a rogue state, at least throughout my own lifetime, but if we look back at the genocide of the Native Americans, followed by the heavy reliance upon slave labor, it is hard to imagine a time when it wasn't an embarrassment to be an American. When I traveled internationally during the post-Vietnam war years, I had to pretend I was Canadian to be socially accepted anywhere.

These days, when there are riots over the pulling down of statues of Robert E. Lee and other figures of the Civil War, it is well to remember, as some commentators have mentioned, that George Washington and Thomas Jefferson were not only slave owners, but, by all accounts, stern if not cruel masters, and clearly racist. One apologist says that, yes, they were slave owners and racist, but they founded this great country. Excuse me – which "great country" are we talking about? Genocide and slavery have been followed by an almost constant parade of wars in perpetuation, not of "Democracy" (Heaven forbid) but of Free Market Capitalism. An international poll has found that the perception is nearly universal that the United States is the greatest threat to world peace – by far – followed by

Pakistan, at a distant second place. A ranking of countries on the basis of social justice placed the United States in twenty-seventh place out of thirty-one, right above Greece, Chile, Mexico, and Turkey.

If anyone is interested in further histories of how the United States has deliberately subverted democratically elected governments in order to install puppet dictators "friendly to American business interests," there are plenty of sources for that information.

Well, let us all spend a few minutes wringing our hands in grief, but then let us consider what is to be done about the elephant in the room. (I was going to say, "what is to be done about the clown in the room," but the problem goes way beyond Donald Trump.)

Many people have already figured it out, notably Osama bin Laden, and the leadership of China. What they have figured out is that military strength is no longer an accurate measure of ultimate power. Power, these days, is measured in money. In other articles, I think I have discussed the idea of "money" as a universal abstraction which can be used to understand, explain, and treat social, political, or environmental problems. So here, for instance, we have the United States as a rogue state rampaging around the world as a gang of outlaw cowboys, led by "Donnie the Kid." But the United States is also a financial corporation, and the key to the problem is that the United States is ultimately insolvent.

So the way to stop Uncle Sam in his tracks is to **call in the loans.** Simply decline to renew the Notes when they come due, and stop accepting Uncle Sam's funny paper. If investors refuse to extend any more credit to the United States corporation, then rates will sky-rocket until someone is willing to invest in the failing state. (Cash out your dollars too, by the way.) And those who do try to profit by investing in "the full faith and credit of the United States government," will most likely lose their money, unless they get out before the final crash.

That's right – *How about a Run on Uncle Sam?* The truth is that Uncle Sam is hopelessly insolvent and can't possibly withstand such a run. Carlo Ponzi survived for a surprisingly long time when there was a run on his bank, but since his bank was fundamentally way beyond unsound (very much like the U.S. government), his "bank" collapsed in the end.

Now what? What does the Post-Apocalyptic world look like, and where do we go from here? Well, I have spelled it all out in my article "A One-World Total Makeover." One hint is to buy land. Don't be caught holding money when the music stops.

The Soviet Union was able to collapse without descending into the chaos of nuclear war; let us hope that the leaders of the bankrupt USA will have the grace to do the same, allowing the people of the earth to evolve a new political and economic structure to carry the world along, as this new millennium unfolds into the future.

A Solution to the Fiasco
of North Korea

September, 2017

I suggest to Kim Jong-un that he should issue a personal challenge to President Donald Trump to a duel: chess boards at three paces, perhaps a single game of chess, the terms of which should be that if Kim Jong-un wins, then the United States takes its toys and goes home: lifts all sanctions, brings its troops home from the Pacific Region, and allows the North Koreans to arrange their own affairs; but if Donald Trump wins the game, then Kim Jong-un will step down, and allow Uncle Sam to set up any puppet government of its choosing in his place.

No matter who wins, it would be a great relief to have this settled. All international disputes, in these days of nuclear weapons, should be submitted to the ordeal by chessboard. My first thought was that each country might designate a champion, and the date for the match set six months ahead, but that were to miss the point: the challenge from Korea is a personal confrontation between the parties, and can only be decided by the principles, not the seconds.

There are many other ways in which this international itching point between equally unstable belligerents might play out, but some of those might be less benign than the ordeal by chessboard.

Geopolitics

October, 2017

Of course the world is a mess, and I have been proposing my solutions for these problems for many years – the establishment of an international Seminary for the education of a special class of selected students who would select one of their number (after a lifetime of studying global issues with the best teachers it is possible to find) to make any final decisions at the apex of the pyramid of authority.

But then I have been going beyond the general argument to consider specific world problems. The centerpiece of my current thinking is to set up my map of world energy patterns at *www.earthflame.org* as a starting point to see the pattern of a huge region around the Middle East where the lowest level of consciousness, the Red-Violet energies, was raging most fiercely.

Well, today I took a look at the map in my world atlas that showed the distribution of religions around the world. They were mostly contiguous regions (in many cases following the lines of language distribution as shown on another map).

I guess it shouldn't have come as such a revelation to me that my two maps so perfectly coincided. The map showing the dominant coverage of Islam just about neatly surrounded this area of maximum global trouble. It is not considered politically correct to make any general value statements about any religious belief or practice. "Of course we are not 'at war with Islam' – the extremists and terrorists and jihadists certainly do not represent Islam, which is a religion of peace and submission to Allah." And yet the circumstantial evidence begins to pile up. Islamic scholars might persuade you that Islam were as peaceful as Buddhism, or at least as peaceful as current expressions of Christianity (distancing ourselves from regrettable crimes committed in the name of Jesus Christ), but all of the action on the ground appears to present a different picture.

In a much earlier article on religion, I concluded that both Islam and Judaism had fundamental problems, as expressions of a relatively primitive understanding of the nature of religious belief. Hinduism and Buddhism seemed much more elevated, spiritually. Christianity, too, shows a remarkably advanced understanding of the main point of religion, although the literature of Christianity is very thin in explaining how to obtain "Christ Consciousness."

So here is my latest solution to the wars in the Middle East – if all the Jews were to become Christian (embracing the gospel of love, and admitting that there is One God over all of us, and there is no "special relationship" with the tribe of Abraham), and all the Moslems were to become Buddhist, seeking peace within, then all problems on the planet would melt away like last year's snow, and all the warring parties could go back to their gardens, their wives (and/or significant others), and their children.

Korean Re-Unification

November, 2017

Whenever I consider a problem and search for solutions, I always want to go to the root of the problem, not wherever the problem appears to obtrude itself, like a neurotic tumor. In the case of North Korea, it seems apparent even obvious, that the fundamental issue, which must be addressed before any other measures can have any realistic effect, is the Korean Divide. First, Korea must be re-united as a single nation; then it may begin the slow process of re-integration into the world community.

So here is my suggested solution – both North and South Korea can agree to set up a Unification School somewhere along the borders of their countries. Each side would select perhaps eight students, four boys and four girls, at about the age of ten years, but not taken from any notable families. These sixteen students would be provided with the best education possible, at State expense. Each side would be allowed to provide half the curriculum. These students would then be prepared for a time, perhaps when the youngest reaches the age of thirty, when these students would select one of their number to head a government over the whole of Korea, setting up such political and economic and social arrangements as they see fit, and nominating their choices of personnel to supervise the various administrative functions. By the time this transfer of power were effected (over the span of about twenty years), both sides would have become prepared for the change, and it should happen smoothly, as the advantages of unification would greatly outweigh any considerations about how the selected Guardian of a new Korea might interpret his or her mandate.

Six Regions of the World
on the Way to World Union

November, 2017

I think a lot about geo-politics. I have figured out how to establish a source of Authority, coming from God, by establishing a Seminary of Candidates who would, upon reaching their majority, choose one of their number to take responsibility from the top (as, for example, the Advocate for the Tree of the Church of the Living Tree). This is a very old idea of mine.

But suppose that happens, and we set up our new Bank and Currency, and set out to restore the earth to a flourishing organic garden of life once again, starting with the immediate planting of millions and billions of trees. But the earth is a big place, with many languages, races, and religions. "Something is lost, and something is gained." Of course, there must be one universal language world-wide, and English is the obvious choice. But the advancement and teaching of the English language should still be greatly accelerated so that the very next generation, world-wide, will be already largely fluent in English.

But I haven't yet gotten to today's idea – I want to extend the seminary idea to at least the next level down. I start by dividing the world up into significant regions, such as:

Region	*Common Tongue*
1.) East Asia to India	(Chinese/English)
2.) Islam from Pakistan to Turkey	(Arabic)
3.) Europe	(English)
4.) Africa	(English)
5.) South America up to Mexico	(Spanish)
6.) USA and Canada	(English)

Each region would have a regional Bank office that would distribute funds for that region, and a Governor, chosen by the regional seminary, who would execute direction by the authority delegated from the Advocate.

A congress of representatives from every part of each region would meet and deliberate current affairs. These might be democratically elected from each local region, at a level where democracy can be most effective.

The regions I have indicated above by common language show three regions where English is not dominant – areas of Chinese, Arabic, and Spanish speaking people. The language people speak is a critical distinction between people. As I look over my six regions, I see most of them on an easy transition to English, with the Spanish region and the French a generation later to adopt English. No one need abandon his own language – everyone will speak at least two languages, his own native language and English. The region of China and India will have no trouble adopting English – the Chinese want to dominate the world, and they will understand that that means learning English.

Africa has always been a basket case, but with a regional Governor, things might settle down.

So that leaves Arabia and the Middle East with no interest in learning English or giving up Islam. I am struck by an idea I have been having lately with my earthflame.org idea – that when all the colors have been mapped out on the globe, with a few exceptions, most of the lowest scores (well into the Red and Violet) all seem to cluster around this same regional area. Even North Korea is likely to subside without violence, as long as cool heads prevail and allow a Mexican stand-off.

So, not to be alarmist, but I see no lasting and insoluble political problems other than the endless hotbed of the Middle East, with Israel right there in the middle, and endless conflict all around. I thought my earlier idea was a great one, if only tongue-in-cheek – that all the Jews should convert to Christianity, and all the Moslems should convert to Buddhism – what a neat solution!

I think there is a vortex of negative energy, like a magnetic field, with its negative pole in the Middle East. Then I figured that if it had the same physics as a magnetic field, the opposite pole would be in the vacant middle of the South Pacific Ocean.

Well, here is a big surprise – I am predicting that the Middle East will continue to be the most troublesome and volatile region of the planet for the foreseeable future. What to do about it? Is it possible that a product of the Arabian Seminary could keep the peace in his (or her, but not likely) region? I don't know if it will work, but I think the division of the planet into those six regions, with a Governor elected by each Seminary, is the most progressive solution yet proposed. Just as the Spanish region and France will be a generation later adopting English, it will probably take about four or five generations for Arabia to settle down and accept the English language.

Another possibility is that Arabia will always remain in opposition to the rest of the world. That seems like a real possibility. They may even never come to accept the authority of the Advocate, but remain totally in opposition. Metaphysically, this outcome may be necessary and inevitable.

The Apple of Discord

December, 2017

The Apple of Discord, from Homeric myth (*"to the fairest"* – Helen of Troy), is the same as the fruit of the Tree of the Knowledge of Good and Evil. "In the day ye eat thereof, then your eyes shall be opened, and ye shall be as gods, knowing good and evil." (Genesis 3:5)

There are many ways to express the original ideas of yang and yin, SOLVE ET COAGULA, expand and contract, etc., but an interesting one, from the point of view of social philosophy, is the distinction between Sharpeners and Levelers. The history of social and economic movement can be seen very clearly as the progressive interplay between sharpeners and levelers. When it comes to politics, Left and Right don't really explain it – are you a Sharpener or a Leveler? For example, one problem of the Jews is that they have always been considered excessive sharpeners. Fascism, as it seems to be used lately, is just extreme sharpening. I was listening to a talk on fascism recently, and the speaker mentioned the line, "equality is a myth." Are we all equal, or what?

But that's the whole essence of the problem. The leveler says, "we are all equal to anyone else on the planet." The sharpener says, "Behold, I will separate the sheep from the goats (– knowing good and evil)."

Alternative to the view that we are all equal, is the view that, on the contrary, there is a great amount of variance which may be observed on many levels of value among people of the world. This was widely taken for granted a century ago and earlier, but by now social, economic, and demographic changes have created a whole new world. So, the world is changing; that much is clear. But is this a good thing or not? And where is it going to go from here?

Any program for the reversal of the imminent death of most life on the planet will have to include planting trees, and limiting or reducing the number of people on the planet. The earth has exceeded its carrying capacity many years ago, and is now raging out of control due to the devastating loss of the trees, and the corresponding growth of people.

The biological health of our planet can be measured by the growth of the trees. When our forests and trees were at their fullest extent, our planet was at its greatest health, biologically, and it has been declining in health ever since. And now our planet is dying because so many of the trees are gone. – and the topsoil is gone; and the small animals are gone; and the human race is on the way out. Not only must we restore tree cover to the earth, and do so very quickly, but the whole planet must be cultivated as a garden. Our lives must be in tune with the garden all the time, and in every way. All food sold must be organically grown; chemical fertilizers must give way to organically derived processes, etc.

It will take a long time to repair the biological health of the planet – perhaps a couple of centuries at least to recover, even if a huge tree-planting effort were immediately under way. It is a lot easier and faster to destroy a forest than it is to grow it back.

So, how can there be any process by which it may be decided, and by whom, how the next generation of people on the planet can be limited? Who will be allowed to have children, and how many? Any attempt to apply an idea to this task will be met with overwhelming obstacles. So, finally, it can only proceed according to that universal abstraction, Money, as the vehicle of regulation. That means just what it sounds like it means – that if you have the financial resources to raise children, you will be able to do so. Those who do not have such resources will refrain from having children, if having children would be a financial burden.

This is a policy and a trend that will work its way out very gradually over the years (as it has already been going on for many years now), and there is, of course, a very obvious Darwinism about this.

But that is where the State comes in, to limit and regulate the sharpeners, and provide leveling solutions for everyone else. In December of 2017, the Trump Reality Show trundles along, hurtling the country and the world who knows where? The sharpeners are way out of control here.

And yet, it is consternating for me to follow the career of Hun Sen of Cambodia, who is on his way to becoming perpetual despot and tyrant. If I go back to my serene and idyllic beach in Cambodia, it will be under a regime as bogus as anything the Moron-in-Chief can throw at us over here. As I look around the world, almost every regime is totally corrupt, but the problem with the Donald is that he presides over a country with enough power to destroy the world.

Good luck, poor little planet.

The world needs an international leveler to take out such loose cannons as Donald Trump, Netanyahu, Erdogan, Hun Sen, Duterte, etc.

The situation of the earth is getting more desperate with each passing day, no thanks to the climate change deniers or war mongers. We are literally living through the death throes of the planet, as it is unable to cope first with the devastating loss of the trees, and then with the onslaught of all those people and their increasingly dangerous toys. The fabric of life is breaking down in so many parts of the world, as our planet hurtles out of control. If there is to be any hope at all of reversing this slide into chaos and oblivion, the whole earth, with its trees, plants, animals, and people, must be cultivated as a single garden, and there must be one Gardener, who derives his authority from God, who will survey the whole earth and its living systems for the good of all.

Requiem for a Lost Planet

April, 2018

It is so frustrating for me to sit here in my cabin in the mountains listening to the news every day, detailing the ongoing collapse and death of the earth. All the same ideas keep going through my head, but I've said it all before – many times over. On the physical level, the greatest problem is the loss of the trees of our poor planet earth. On the social and political level, the greatest problem is the absence of any coherent source of authority. What we need is a political union of the entire earth, followed by an immediate and massive program of tree planting. But it will take hundreds of years of planting trees to restore essential tree cover to the planet, and there are just too many people on the earth for there to be any room to plant the trees that are needed. People have replaced trees on our planet, to the great sorrow of the earth (She is alive, and feels the pain). The human race is like a parasite on the earth which is rapidly destroying the host. Some observers have estimated that the last chance to slow and reverse this slide unto death was passed about sixty years ago, and that by now the collapse of our ecosystem is irreversible. So, eat, drink, and be merry, for tomorrow we die.

Perhaps it is already too late, but isn't it better to make some effort anyway? Perhaps an intensive program of change may yet add an extra ten years onto the short time we have left before all life on earth finally crumbles into dust. But, instead of a concerted world-wide effort to slow down the destruction of the earth, we see escalating political chaos which threatens to destroy the earth even sooner, through the action of "fire and fury." The world may finally end not with a whimper, but with a bang, after all.

It is too late and useless to plan for some world-wide revolution that might make a change. I figure that the only hope is for the holders of wealth and power to get together to implement a new vision for the earth. I have expressed my views about how this can be done many times, and I am not going to revisit any of that here. So then there is nothing to say, except to express my frustration and sorrow that such a beautiful earth, the only known planet manifesting such an explosively rich diversity of life, must be lost to the folly of the human race.

I remember that some fifty years ago there was a forlorn hope that perhaps some remnant of the human race might leave the earth in spaceships to establish life on some other planet. Perhaps a modern day Ark could contain seeds and at least a few animals together with a selection of the human race, and head off into the wild black yonder in hopes of finding another hospitable host where that remnant of life could try to reestablish itself. I seem to remember that the unappreciated visionary, Timothy Leary, was one of the principle advocates of such an exodus as the last hope of that field of life energy we have come to understand as Gaia. ("Turn on, tune in, and drop out," and then do something new – my interpretation of Leary's famous slogan.)

But such a desperate gamble would seem to have an extremely low probability of success. Perhaps, after all, the best remaining hope for life on earth is still to try to salvage something from the wreckage of our planet so that some sort of life might continue to live on this earth, even if the chance that the human race might form a part of that life seems vanishingly slim.

The threat of a nuclear Winter (without any hope of a Spring any time soon) is the greatest threat to life, but there are other threats almost as severe – the increasing spread of toxic chemical waste that is still being distributed over the planet by the likes of such criminals as the directors of the Monsanto corporation – arguably more heinous criminals than Hitler ever was, to say nothing of the rapacious villainy of the banksters, whose depredations are almost harmless in comparison with those who are rendering the entire earth uninhabitable and toxic to life. The increasing spread of the sickness of cancer is the prime symptom of the declining health and vitality of the earth. This is widely understood, yet no one seems to have any idea of what is to be done about it. Of course, I've laid it all out, but no one ever listens to me. Donald Trump is not the problem – he is just a symptom of the problem – that the United States has followed the course exactly predicted by Thomas Jefferson at the founding of that country (not *my* country – I disavow association with that stinking corruption). "The longer any system of government goes on, the more the wealth and power will be concentrated in fewer and fewer hands," Jefferson declared, and that is exactly what has been happening, as is glaringly evident to anyone who takes off their emerald glasses long enough to see what is really happening in the land of Oz. Thomas Jefferson also just as clearly expressed the only solution – that a new revolution is necessary every twenty-seven years (the "re-set button").

But I am repeating themes I first expressed forty years ago, and I am trying not to just repeat the same old tunes. But what else is there to do? Lock the emerald glasses onto our heads and eat, drink, and be merry, for tomorrow we die.

Weapons of War

April, 2018

I don't even remember where, or when, or how often I have remarked on the very troubling fact that nothing is made in the USA anymore; everything is made in China – with one very troubling exception: weapons. Today, on the news, Donald Trump is being called the world's preeminent weapons salesman, as he gloats over his record of promoting the sale of American made weapons all over the globe. The problem with that is that the American economy flourishes in direct proportion to the prevalence of war and rumors of war worldwide. In the event of a period of relative peace on earth, the American economy would plummet disastrously, while the rest of the world, led by China, would enjoy a period of increasing prosperity. The implications of this *consideratum* are inescapable. When this situation is added to the historical perspective that the last manifestations of an aging and dying empire are typically a resort to military adventurism, it is clearly time to book seats on Timothy Leary's rocket ship into outer space in search of new pastures for the survivors of the human race fleeing from Armageddon (see previous article, *Requiem for a Lost Planet*).

There is nowhere to go to be safe from the fallout patterns after a Nuclear Winter. Perhaps you might consider the Southern Hemisphere, far away from the major land masses of Australia, Africa, and South America, and settle upon some South Sea island as your best hope. Unfortunately, the effects of global warming will mean that those islands will all soon be under water. But, perhaps, with the advance of global warming, by the time that the last South Sea islands are sinking into the sea, a warming Antarctica may become relatively habitable. I suggest that the smart money will quickly get enough settlements established there to declare the continent to be a sovereign nation, with vast tracts of land doled out to the early settlers as speculations for a future land rush. I remember a funny cartoon about a real estate agent showing "Lakeside Condominia" to prospective buyers: "Oh, I guess the lake isn't in yet." I know the joke is ruined by my insistence on the Latin plural, but I just can't help it.

Anyway, you heard it here first – if there are any human survivors on this planet, the descendants of the early colonists on Antarctica will be living high on the hog. Perhaps we should set up some gambling casinos and regulated brothels to jump-start tourism. However, most projections only give such "safe havens" an extra year or two before the inexorable tide of death supervenes everywhere.

Sorry if I seem to be descending into cynical pessimism these days (I used to be an optimist, expecting the human race to pull itself out of the spiraling descent into chaos at the last minute), but it's hard to see any bright spots. I am reminded of the computer simulated war games – *no matter what start-up assumptions are programmed into the computer,* every single simulation always ends up with the annihilation of all life on earth. No wonder there's an "opioid crisis" – whatever you do, stay away from the psychedelics – stick to the opioids or that standard of despair, alcohol. Ease the pain of the end of life on earth with a bottle of absinthe, and go out happy.

Meditation on Consciousness

April, 2018

Frequently, in my philosophical speculations, I don't know which way to apply symbolic representations of yang and yin. The issue is greatly clarified by the concepts of Young Yang, Young Yin, Old Yang, and Old Yin from the I Ching. Thus we have the All and Nothing of the Old Yang and Old Yin, but there is also the expanding and contracting of the Young Yang and Young Yin. But then the issue is further complexified by the concept of *enantiodromia*, that the consequence of the extreme of either yang or yin is a reversal into its opposite direction.

But another consideration that I run into repeatedly is that, given any microcosm (or Macrocosm, for that matter, as a good Hermeticist), while some aspects are expanding as yang, others are contracting as yin. Thus, for example, we have the world exploding into astonishing levels of complexity, typified by the apparently limitless potential of computers and the internet. One thing is for sure – we haven't seen anything yet. The whole computer and internet age is just in its veriest infancy. But this has divergent consequences – some of the consequences are very good, while others are very bad. One simple example is the unbelievable access to information. In so many ways, this opens up whole new worlds of possibility, accelerating the pace of advancing science and technology, but it also means the total end of privacy as we know it. Children are now being born into a world where everything is known about everything and everyone, and plenty of people seem to welcome this development, or at least accept it as the inevitable price of our unprecedented access to information.

Other developments are a bit more sinister – "the more theoretical control is gained, the more actual control is lost." For example, chemical pesticides and herbicides may seem to augment the capacity of the earth to grow more food to feed more people (arguably, not at all a good thing on the face of it), but, in fact, they may be destroying the ecosystem of the earth, killing off not only harmful insects, but beneficial insects as well. Bees are massively dying off, and the deaths of people to cancer, caused by our increasingly toxic world environment, are not far behind. And, *quod erat demonstrandum*, modern technology may create incredibly powerful nuclear weapons, but, rather than making the world more secure, they threaten to destroy all life on earth.

Change happens slowly, too slowly to notice. Personal privacy is not the only thing that is being lost to the modern world. Many of today's young people know nothing of trees, gardens, or fresh food. Four-fifths of every supermarket consists of products which I don't recognize as food, from sugary drinks to processed "food." And hamburgers are not only destroying the last of the ancient rainforests (one of the major sources of pollution is the smoke from the thousands of acres of rainforest burned off every day to make room for more burger-beef), but they are also destroying the health of anyone so misguided as to eat them, thinking they are a kind of food, washed down with sugar water and greasy fries.

But none of this was what was on my mind when I took up my pencil today (I am happy to edit by computer, but I compose by pencil, an ancient wooden artifact filled with carbon, formerly used for writing before the advent of computers).

I wanted to discuss consciousness. I have been using the imagery of spiritual elevation leading to convergence at a center of unity, clarity, cosmic consciousness, love, joy, and health. Distance from this center leads out progressively into error, disharmony, subject-object divergence, anger, and conflict, leading finally to chaos, darkness, and death. But there is an aspect of consciousness that increases as a function of complexity – higher organisms, representing increased orders of complexity, exhibit greater consciousness. How do I reconcile those concepts? Isn't the expansion into complexity the pattern of moving away from the perfection at the center? But "a little knowledge leads one away from God; a greater knowledge brings one back, closer to God." This is a case of two movements in different directions going on at once – the yang energy of separation and expansion into diversity, and the yin energy of the coalescence of consciousness back to the center of unity, clarity, and love. These are independent movements – the elevation of consciousness towards unity can be going on in spite of an ongoing expansion into complexity.

I don't have a finished idea to present here; that's why I call it a meditation.

I think where I'm going with this is that some "New Age" writers seem to assert that the ultimate origin of the universe is pure consciousness, from which all manifestation has been derived. This has a really nice "feel good" aspect about it – you know, the Original Mind of God as the Creator of the universe. But as I look back on my theological speculations, I seem to have been suggesting a more impersonal explanation for the origin of the universe, that the universe somehow "created itself" – came into being spontaneously as an inevitable manifestation of ultimate *a priori* principles (*vide: The Evolution of Theology, Speculations on Cosmic Consciousness and the Love of God,* and *Philosophical Meditations on the Nature of God*). Then, not only is consciousness a later development, but God Herself is evolving along with Her Cosmos. In other words, until and unless we find some more evolved beings somewhere, as far as we know, We are the cutting edge of Consciousness, and God and Gaia are evolving along with us. This is a total reversal of most New Age doctrine, but it makes more sense to me.

In many ways, I think I am getting at what Pierre Teilhard de Chardin was talking about as we expand our evolutionary growth of consciousness towards an unknowable Omega Point (*vide: The Phenomenon of Man* by Teilhard de Chardin). This evolution of life and consciousness is still going on. Compare the evolution of Man's understanding of God, from the very primitive, vengeful, and petty God of the Old Testament (not welcome at my house; if the Old Testament God were to show up at my house, I would offer Him a meal and a place to sleep, out of Christian charity, but then send Him on down the road), to the far more enlightened God of Love of the New Testament, to present conceptions of Gaia, encompassing not just the tribe of Hebrews, nor even the whole human race, but the entire field of life energy on the planet.

Human consciousness, too, is evolving on all sides. Perhaps the Omega Point of Teilhard de Chardin represents the convergence back to the center of unity, clarity, love, and light which enlightened mystics have been describing for a long time. Perhaps one day a critical mass of enlightenment will propel the human race, along with all life on earth, towards a new Golden Age.

Let us hope that the energy towards such a convergence will overtake and displace the contrary energy towards divergence, destruction, and chaos which is riding us rampantly (transitive verb) to the edge of darkness.

Gravity

May, 2018

I have briefly mentioned my idea of gravity as the yin force of a "return to the center" which balances the yang force of the "quest for novelty" (*Speculations on the Nature of God*, 3.III.15), but I want to take a closer look at it today.

One of the fundamental questions which continue to bother scientists and philosophers is, "Why is there any universe here at all, instead of just nothing?" I have also been confused by that problem, and my solution is not altogether satisfying even to me (that the universe just popped into being spontaneously, in accordance with some inevitable ultimate reality).

But I don't want to belabor that problem anymore here – what I want to do is to accept those two opposing forces as given, and try to understand how those two forces might explain the nature of the cosmos as we know it.

I start by agreeing that the "natural" state of the cosmos is nothingness, non-being, *ain soph*. This is not yet "zero" – zero is already far along on the road to the manifestation of being. Now comes the "Laughter of God" (or however you like to express this mystery) which separates nothingness into two parts, All and Nothing, or an expansive force which creates and maintains a subject/object distinction, and a complementary force which resolves all such distinctions back to "the center" (the singularity which started and/or ended it all).

I am happy to see that some recent speculations on the nature of the cosmos tend to see some sort of endless cycle expanding out of a singularity and finally resolving back into a black hole, whence it might re-emerge to form a "new universe." This has always made more sense to me than the facile postulation of an original Big Bang *ex nihilo*. However we may wish to explain the expansive force, or attempt to account for its presence or existence, it is clear to me that the opposite force, of reduction back to the center, from diversity back to singularity, is what we know of as the force of gravity.

Since nothingness is the "natural" state of the cosmos, some force or intervention is required to create and maintain a distinction. One of my earliest philosophical pronouncements (dating back to my book of *Jokes*, 1975, letterpress, miniature) is "Time is the Measure of Error." I might slightly update that pronouncement as: "Time and Space are the Measures of Error." Thus, the expansive yang energy of subject/object distinction is identified as some sort of error, like the grain of sand in an oyster which generates a pearl. So, as that initial force dissipates, and the distinctions resolve back to singularity, the manifestations of time and space tend to return back to zero. (A singularity, as a point of no dimensions, is indistinguishable from zero, the reverse of the First Arcanum, which refers to the emergence of the Singularity from the Zero Arcanum of *ain soph*.)

This whole process of the return back to the singularity is what is observed as the "force of gravity." That is, the "force of gravity" isn't really a force, at all; it is just the dissipation of the contrary force which generates expansion into proliferating distinction. In other words, yang expresses an active force reaching out into novelty and distinction, while yin is the passive return to the equilibrium of nothingness. The Hermetic alchemists summed up the whole process as SOLVE ET COAGULA.

So, is everything clear now? Of course I have side-stepped the whole question of the origin, nature, and meaning of that yang force of distinction, the quest for novelty. Words are wholly inadequate (which is why I resort to quotation marks so often), but to suggest that the whole "Laughter of God" is somehow based on some sort of error, or "crack in the cosmic egg," seems to me to be hinting, in some poetical fashion, for an interpretation of the ultimate mystery of why there is anything here at all, instead of just nothingness.

The Religion Taboo

August, 2018

Continuing along the line of the observation that if we draw a map of the world in which every area is colored according to my scheme of aura colors, then there is a startling overlap of the most volatile areas, in the colors of Red and Purple, with the range of Islam over the globe. But that's not the Islam I know – isn't Islam all about peace and obedience to the Will of Allah? So why is the face of Islam so mired in the Red of aggression and violence, and the Purple of oppression and defeat?

I know that it is not considered politically correct to question another person's religion, but I have found that, even though all religions speak of similar themes, there seem to be differences among the major religions that suggest to me sorting them out according to the colors of their aura. This is a pretty radical political venture. It suggests that there are differences in spiritual or ethical value among the religions of the world: that some are better than others.

All of the placement of the colors seems to be obvious, except perhaps the Orange of Hinduism, but I see Hinduism as a religion of engagement with the world, where Buddhism is a religion of withdrawal from the world (Blue). Christianity has always been the clearest voice for the message of love (Yellow). The Jews have historically been oppressed people (Purple), while Moslems seem to be on an endless jihad (Red).

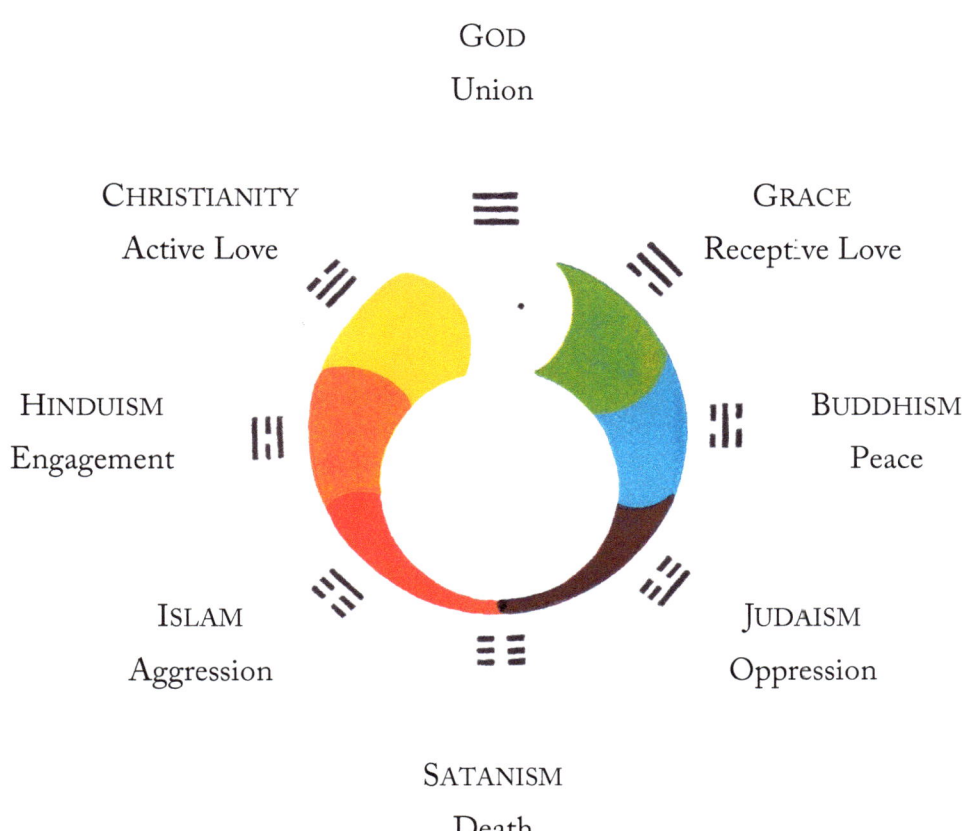

So here it is possible to see the levels of value, with the Black of Satanism on the bottom, and the Jews and Moslems slugging it out, literally, on the line between life and death, with Hinduism and Buddhism at a clearly elevated plane of consciousness above. This puts Christianity close to the top, along with the Grace of God (Yellow and Green). Above is the merger into Cosmic Consciousness at the apex of Union (White).

I am just sitting here stunned at the extent to which this is all politically incorrect. How can I sit here and make these judgments? Well, I just call them as I see them, and I find Christianity to be the clearest expression of the highest religious experience. Leaving aside Hinduism and Buddhism, both of which impart valuable spiritual values to their followers, that leaves Islam and Judaism as problematic religions, and I look at them not through their theology, but through the actions of their adherents. I find them both to be primitive (somewhere on the level of the Old Testament God). Someone should send missionaries to spread the message of higher levels of experience.

Well, intellectual honesty compels me to acknowledge that I do not believe that all religions are equally worthy of respect, but that some are better than others (from the point of view of world harmony). I have eaten fearlessly from the fruit of the Tree of the Knowledge of Good and Evil, the Apple of Discord. According to Homeric myth, the Apple of Discord was the source of the origin of the cosmos, which I call "The Laughter of God."

As I look over what I wrote yesterday, I see that it is deeply flawed. I have been critical of both Islam and Judaism, not because of their theology or stated principles, but because of the way the people live their lives. Obviously this is a gross generalization – I am just reacting to what I see on the ground, and that is the unconscionable behavior of the Israelis towards the Palestinians as they pursue the "final solution" to the "Palestinian problem" without any appreciation of the historical irony, and the endless jihad of Moslems all over the globe. I must, in fairness, dissociate the State of Israel from the Jewish people worldwide, most of whom seem to live their lives innocuously enough.

However, in the case of Christianity, I have focused on the essence of what it is all about, rather than the actions of Christians. But even if we only look at the present day, and ignore all of the historical atrocities committed in the name of Jesus Christ, the picture is not unequivocal. The United States is predominately Christian, overall, yet its government is out of control in planetary-wide life-threatening depravity. Perhaps it is more accurate to characterize the United States as essentially lacking in any religious awareness at all. In any case, it is very hard to find any uniform standards by which to compare the integrity of religious beliefs.

I guess I have to conclude that my catalog of religious beliefs according to the predominant aura color is just an idle amusement which cannot be seriously defended. But it is useless to consider the value of religious teaching while neglecting the way that teaching influences the moral expression of its adherents.

I wrote all of that several days ago, and I have been unhappy about it ever since. At the very least, we will have to say that it is grossly oversimplified, if not entirely misleading and worthless. And yet, something about the idea persists, and I just can't let it go. The basic problem is that it deliberately targets both Jews and Moslems as living under a substandard religious influence, with negative consequences.

But, if that is the core of the issue, perhaps there is something to it. As I look at what I know of Judaism and Islam (and I take my knowledge not from their sacred literature and traditions, but from an observance of the effect of their religion on personal behavior), I have to say that I don't see much of any tendency to love thy neighbor. Islam gets points for their hospitality to strangers and travelers, and I have always felt that one of the most charming traditions of Judaism is the Seder, some special memorial dinner in which one is urged to find someone who is alone and invite him to share the meal together with your family. I also want to mention that I have traveled extensively in Moslem countries and I have encountered numerous instances of very friendly people who have gone out of their way to be helpful to me, and I have never personally witnessed any moral shortcomings of the Moslem people. But that still leaves the unimaginable depravity of the State of Israel against the Palestinian people, and the endless jihad of Moslems, mostly against other Moslems, not just against The Great Satan and other Western countries. If it is unfair of me to malign these religions on the basis of the actions of some minority of their adherents, I would say that is up to the religious leaders of both Judaism and Islam to speak out against those abuses and clarify the position of their faith. *Place your bets here:* will the leaders of Judaism be the first to speak out against the State of Israel, or will the leaders of Islam speak out against the endless wars carried on in the name of Islam?

On the whole, Christianity is way out in front expressing the high ground of spiritual consciousness. *"A new commandment I give unto you, that ye love one another; as I have loved you, that ye also love one another. By this shall all men know that ye are my disciples, if ye have love one to another."* (John XIII: 34-35)

Now I want to get down to cases. First of all, levels of spiritual consciousness contain both sides in their aura – Yellow and Green, Orange and Blue, and Red and Purple. I have placed the Moslems on the Red side, and Jews on the Purple side, but in the case of the relationship between the Jews and the Palestinians in Israel/Palestine, the Jews are clearly the violent aggressors (Red), and the Palestinians are the oppressed victims (Purple). I have seen as a general observation of human nature that when someone commits an injustice upon someone else, rather than apologize for their error, they double-down and increase their violent attacks against their victim. Here, the Israelis are clearly exhibiting the characteristic behavior of persons ruled by a Red/Purple aura, which typically oscillates between aggression and violence on the one hand, and then further oppression as victim on the other. It is a vicious cycle that can only be transcended by going upwards.

More and more I am thinking that my "facetious" suggestion that Jews should convert to Christianity and Moslems to Buddhism is literally the way forward in this thousand year old conflict in the Middle East. If the Jews were suddenly visited with Christ Consciousness (like Saul on the road to Damascus), they might make a sudden leap upwards in spiritual consciousness, open their borders to returning Palestinians, end all embargo by sea, rebuild the infrastructure that they have been so persistently demolishing for the last hundred years, and offer cash reparations to Palestinians who have been forcibly removed from their land. If they were to do all of this, then relations between the Jews and Palestinians might approach normal conditions in as little as two or three generations. And, as for Moslems embracing Buddhism, I think that would be the best thing for the peace of the earth. They need to try meditation and find peace within;

they need to let go of all of the anger and aggression and return to the love of their families and friends.

Anyway, instead of fighting against any of these people, either Jews or Moslems, they should be offered opportunities of religious education, something like Christian Science Reading Rooms (rather than, for example, more aggressive Missionaries). Whether Jews or Moslems actually convert to Christianity or Buddhism, or whether they just advance new sects which embody higher levels of spiritual awareness and expression, it all amounts to the same thing in the end.

The Holy Ghost

September, 2018

The Holy Ghost is the Cosmic Consciousness of God. In this sense, it is easy to see that the same God which is the entirety of the Cosmic Consciousness of God is also that *Primum Mobile* which caused the cosmos to come into being, bursting out with Novelty as it expands into endless complexity. There are two directions of energy known as God (or God and the Devil) : God as the movement in, back towards the Center, and God as the creative movement outward into Novelty, away from the Center. Altogether it is a Trinity, the understanding of which is the traditional Secret of occult philosophy.

God and Our universe come into being as God divides Himself into yang and yin. SOLVE ET COAGULA.

Uncertainty

October, 2018

Is it a Quest for Novelty or simply the fundamental error rate of the cosmos? In my search for God, I value this reaching out into novelty just as much as I value the return to the Center of Perfection. And I keep wondering (reverently) whence comes this outward quest into novelty? But perhaps it all comes down to the fact that our universe just isn't perfect, after all, but is subject to some mean failure rate. Perhaps there is some small chance that any particle of matter or energy could flip into its opposite expression at any time or at any place. This fundamental uncertainty would be what makes our cosmos lurch along at random, exploding into novelty as it expands.

So, according to this theory, the *primum mobile* is the expression of that inescapable potential for error in the cosmos. At some point in time (which didn't exist until that moment) the Universe slipped out of Perfection and fell into Being. Naturally, there is a powerful force for the restoration of Perfection again (gravity), equal to the energy which broke it apart, but that potential for error in the cosmos just seems to keep pushing the universe further out into complexity. Perhaps, because of that error potential, there is no chance of restoring perfection, or stopping the cosmos from spinning out into ever increasing complexity, finally leading to darkness, chaos, and death. So now I don't know whether the universe will finally contract back to a singularity again (Perfection) or if each universe just plays out until its heat death (the opposite pole of the Singularity) and then we wait for the cosmos to slip out of perfection again some time, falling into Being one more time. *I look, but I see it both ways.*

If the Universe were perfect, it wouldn't exist; existence implies error. But there's a flaw somewhere. Earlier I was writing about incorporating uncertainty into a non-binary logic for a computer. Suppose that at any place, at any time, there is always a chance – very small perhaps, but not zero – that "anything" might reverse into its opposite expression (remembering from Heraclitus that anything or any idea can only exist along with its opposite). Suppose that this is just a fact about our universe here – No; it isn't perfect; there is always the chance that anything could suddenly flip into its opposite expression "without intervention", *i.e.,* without perceivable cause according to the known laws of physics. And perhaps this fundamental Uncertainty is one more of the laws of physics.

The good news is that it is this Error which allows our universe to come into being at all, for which I am thankful and grateful. As for this endless potential for uncertainty, it isn't necessarily bad news – perhaps it is what accounts for the persistent novelty reaching into the Unknown with a new idea, and is responsible for all of the interest in this silly world of ours.

And what if that were the whole idea all along? Perhaps the Consciousness of God came into being with the first event or error. This particular universe with its Conscious God is alive and going on, gathering momentum as it expands. We always knew that nothing could be Perfect – there always has to be some flaw somewhere, or it can't exist.

Proposed Address to the First Convocation of the Seminary of the Church of the Living Tree

October, 2018

We thank all of you for accepting a place in this project of ours. You may still be wondering just what it is we are expecting you to do. Here we are putting together all of the best help we can find to prepare a program that will prepare all of you for the possible role of Advocate for the Tree. Carefully chosen instructors from many fields will be presenting their knowledge and their ideas to you. To begin with, we set up a program and tell you what to do, but, from the founding of this Seminary today, the final authority will always rest with yourselves. While you are young, we expect that you will try to take all of this in respectfully, and try to learn the lessons we are trying to teach you. But the whole function and purpose of the Seminary is for you to figure out what has to happen in this world, and tell us what to do, as soon as you are ready to do so.

For the last two or three centuries, the earth has been showing the wear that the human race has put upon it, and has been declining in biological health. This is a Red Alert for the planet. The biological health of our planet is the whole story as far as the survival of the human race is concerned. There are a host of problems associated with this biological collapse of our biosphere, and every one of those problems will have to be dealt with immediately and decisively – the loss of the Trees worldwide will have to be offset by the largest tree planting effort ever attempted, carrying on the work of people such as Richard St. Barbe Baker, whose efforts for the Trees are gratefully remembered.

The burning off as fuel the last forty million years' worth of the accumulation of fossil fuels will have to be met by capping those wells and closing those mines for the next forty million years, by which time it may be possible to take a sustained yield harvest of some of that material for certain high-value uses, but certainly not to be burned off as fuel, which is a terrible waste, as stupid as cutting down trees to make paper which is then buried as landfill within a few weeks.

War is probably the greatest contributor to climate change – not only from the primary effect of all the bombs, but counting also the secondary effects of the whole war machine and all of the devastation that follows. Resolving disputes through our international court system will finally lay to rest the whole gigantic war industry, which has been physically destroying our earth as well as impoverishing its people for as long as anyone has kept any records. If all of that stops now, our work here will be much easier.

Plant Trees over all of the fields of war, and cultivate all of the earth as a garden.

Endgame, USA?

October, 2018

The United States of America is getting scarier by the minute. Donald Trump is so far beyond belief of what any American President should be that we are off into unchartered territory. The country is almost isolated in the world, left with the likes of Saudi Arabia and Israel among its dwindling circle of friends in the world. Throw in a few more, like Duterte in the Philippines and Erdogan in Turkey, and you have a gang of peers all wallowing in similar troughs of spiritual darkness, all of whom understand each other perfectly well.

But the times, they are a-changing. It may be for the better, or it may be for the worse, but changing it is, and it will probably get worse before it gets better. I hear people talk all the time about the inevitable financial collapse that everyone seems to be expecting, but the collapse has actually been here for a while, and is noticeably accelerating.

All of the "smart money" has realized for some time that the entire "United States Government" is a Ponzi Scheme gone out of control. The U.S. Government is a corporation without any assets, with a debt in excess of $20 trillion, and with an annual operating loss of over a trillion dollars. I wouldn't loan it any money, no matter how much interest they offer to pay, even if they denominate the loan in Chinese Yuan. As for speculating in Dollars, that is a cat on a hot stove.

The widening of the gap between the rich and the poor, along with the impending bankruptcy of the USA, suggest that the United States is playing out its endgame. The wealthy 1% (or fewer, depending on how you count) own all of the property, all of the money, and all of the corporations. The poor have nothing; they have no income; and the country that promised them Social Security no longer has the money to pay; so sorry.

Do you think that the wealthy corporations and individuals who own all of the assets in this country are going to chip in and assume responsibility for the nation's debts? If you believe they will, you are one of those born every minute. (*Now is the time for every good man to come to the aid of his country.* Anyone? Even a good woman? Transgender? How about a thieving and conniving rascal? Anyone? You, Henry Kissinger, are you going to leave your wealth to the government?) Oh, no – if the government falls, that is simply a great opportunity to repudiating the debt. Everyone is still going to need to buy your product, even if your "product" is simply an import agency from China.

Besides, there will always be opportunities all over the world for the savvy investor to make his fortune. China will build factories in this country to take advantage of the cheap labor over here, and then they will sell all their products back to the workers, who will always be in debt to the Company Store, barely able to keep up their rent payments to their 'lords.

But, in the meantime, the dollar will collapse as the United States government continues desperately trying to print and spend its way out of debt. This will all happen very quickly. It will be all over before anyone notices. Loss of confidence happens very suddenly, and once it occurs, it is all over. It will happen in the night, while you sleep.

All of this so far has been the optimistic scenario. But, if some troubling trends continue, it could get very much worse than this. There should be an immediate embargo on all sales of American made weapons beyond its borders. Of course, that would be the last nail in the coffin for the American economy, since weapons sales are about all this country has left for foreign trade. But the United States is complicit in the atrocities of Yemen and Palestine as long as they continue to supply Saudi Arabia and Israel with arms.

The last argument of kings is their cannon (*ultima ratio regis*), and wars of conquest, rape, and pillage are famous pathways to the end of the road for aging empires. I fervently hope that the United States will stand down gracefully, and allow itself to be liquidated in bankruptcy proceedings rather than spiraling down into the continuing fire, confusion, and chaos of endless war.

One reason I want to set up my map of world consciousness (earthflame.org) is to highlight the problem that there is a great variation in the average or prevailing consciousness worldwide. I consider the depressing effect of endless war raging across much of the Middle East and surrounding areas – Syria, Palestine, Iraq, Afghanistan, Yemen. The prevailing low level of spiritual consciousness makes it very hard for anyone living there to experience a level of consciousness much above the prevailing level. And now that that whole region is a smoking war zone with refugees by the millions trying to get out of there to some sweeter land where life is good, we see the problem that immigrants and refugees are less and less welcome in some of these literally greener pastures. The fact is that all of these refugees and immigrants are inexorably lowering the level of spiritual consciousness as they flood over into neighboring lands. They may not all be "rapists and murderers," but they carry the scars and the lasting spiritual damage from their long experience in a spiritual wasteland.

So what is the solution, here? Perhaps it makes more sense for everyone to make a stand where they are – to try to forge a political reality more conducive to leading the human spirit upwards. The problem is how to bring down a corrupt regime from within, when it is held in the grip of war lords and profiteers. But this is why there can be so little hope for life on earth until there be some relief from the top, allowing the people beneath them gradually to lift their lives out of the chaos, darkness, and disease of endless war.

As to what happens next, we need to get there quickly.

I know I've said all this before, but I can't get rid of a problem until it is resolved. I sure wish the human race would figure it out quickly, so I could go back to cultivating my fragrant roses in peace.

Go ahead and plant some Trees.

CPSIA information can be obtained
at www.ICGtesting.com
Printed in the USA
BVFW020344231118
533744BV00021B/272/P